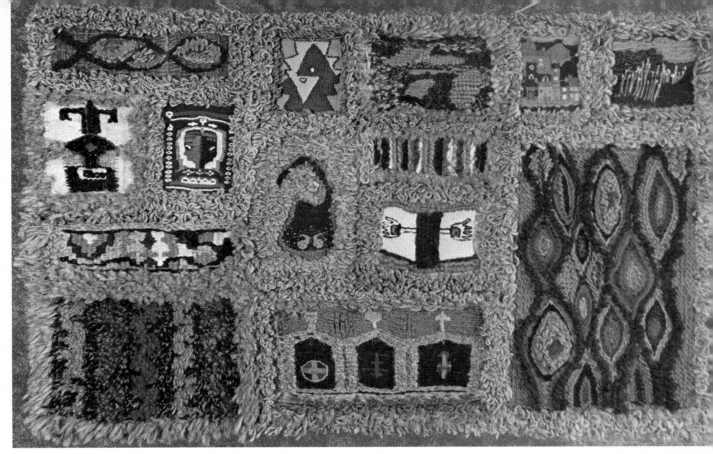

C-1.

C-2.

C-3.

C-4.

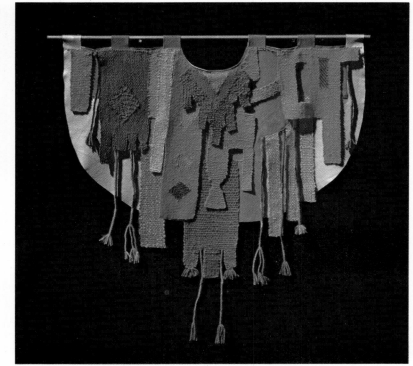

C-7.

C-5.

C-6.

C-8.

C-11.

C-13.

C-12.

C-14.

C-15.

C-16.

C-17.

C-18.

C-19.

C-20.

C-21.

WEAVING YOU CAN USE

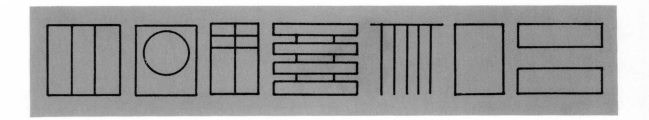

Jean Wilson

VAN NOSTRAND REINHOLD COMPANY
New York Cincinnati London Toronto Melbourne

TO: GARY · SHERI · DAWN

Van Nostrand Reinhold Company Regional Offices:
New York Cincinnati Chicago Millbrae Dallas

Van Nostrand Reinhold Company International Offices:
London Toronto Melbourne

Copyright © 1975 by Litton Educational Publishing, Inc.
Library of Congress Catalog Card Number 74–7778
ISBN 0-442-29547-2 (paper)
ISBN 0-442-29546-4 (cloth)

Designed by Loudan Enterprises
All drawings by Gary Wilson

Published by Van Nostrand Reinhold Company
A Division of Litton Educational Publishing, Inc.
450 West 33rd Street, New York, N.Y. 10001

16 15 14 13 12 11 10 9 8 7 6 5 4 3 2 1

Library of Congress Cataloging in Publication Data

Wilson, Jean Verseput.
  Weaving you can use.

  Bibliography: p.
  Includes index.
  1. Hand weaving.   I. Title.
TT848.W526   746.1'4   74-7778
ISBN 0-442-29546-4
ISBN 0-442-29547-2 pbk.

Books by Jean Wilson

Weaving You Can Use
The Pile Weaves
Weaving You Can Wear
Weaving Is Creative
Weaving Is Fun
Weaving Is for Anyone

COLOR PLATE CAPTIONS

Fig. C-1. The Ethnic Wall Rug's units were woven separately, from different ethnic design sources. By author. (Photograph by Kent Kammerer)

Fig. C-2. Medallion detail from soumak rug. Courtesy of Mr. and Mrs. Harold Tacker. (Photograph by Harold Tacker)

Fig. C-3. The tapestry of a Coptic saint has Greek soumak border. By author. (Photograph by Kent Kammerer)

Fig. C-4. Squares and phantom squares, in glowing colors, characterize this deep pile rug by Mildred Sherwood. (Photograph by Mildred Sherwood)

Fig. C-5. "The Girls" uses tapestry techniques and has a woven border. By author. (Photograph by Kent Kammerer)

Fig. C-6. Eleven-year-old Paul Tsang wove a small bag on a cardboard crescent loom, then wove and applied a pair of bright figures. (Photograph by Harold Tacker)

Fig. C-7. "Flappy Bird" leather and woven wool wall hanging. Weaver: Luana Sever. (Photograph by Beverly Rush)

Fig. C-8. "Old Colonial Comforter" is Luana Severs' updated version of a padded quilt, woven in four sections. (Photograph by Beverly Rush)

Fig. C-9. "Grafics" from four panels planned and woven as a group. By Gloria Crouse. (Photograph by Gloria E. Crouse)

Fig. C-10. A panel folding screen woven to produce a stained-glass window look. By members of the South Coast Weavers' Guild, Santa Ana, California. (Photograph by Curtis and Betty Bell)

Fig. C-11. "Solar Rays," twisting columns of jute and wire, can be an idea for a screening or divider effect. By Marilyn Meltzer. (Photograph by Marilyn Meltzer)

Fig. C-12. Space hanging, woven by Sandra Hastings to partly fill a wide archway.

Fig. C-13. Slit weave and wrapped warps make a walk-through door hanging. Woven by Verla Christianson. (Photograph by Beverly Rush)

Fig. C-14. "Space Weaving" by author. (Photograph by Ron Wilson)

Fig. C-15. These seat pads were shaped on the loom for twin three-legged Mexican chairs. Woven by Joanne Hall. (Photograph by Joanne Hall)

Fig. C-16. Jute and leather hammock, by Marilyn Meltzer. (Photograph by Marilyn Meltzer)

Fig. C-17. Swing in the shade of a tall tree. Woven of jute, leather, and wool, by Marilyn Meltzer. (Photograph by Marilyn Meltzer)

Fig. C-18. These bonus pillows came from unused warp of a burnoose with hood. Woven by Jan Burhen. (Photograph by Jan Burhen)

Fig. C-19. Yellow linen runners are interwoven on the table with a long, narrow Aran Islands sash. Runners by weaver Midge Dodge. (Photograph by Beverly Rush)

Fig. C-20. Tapestry bedspread by the Tacoma Weavers' Guild, Tacoma, Washington.

Fig. C-21. One of the tapestries from the Tacoma spread—Red Mouse. Courtesy Dr. and Mrs. Eugene Lagerberg. (Photographs C-20 and C-21 by Beverly Rush)

Fig. C-22. "Red Quilt." Woven strips, joining seams chainstitched, and card-woven bands join the four assembled sections. By weaver Karen Kaufman. (Photograph by Harold Tacker)

Contents

Acknowledgments

My most sincere thanks to all of you talented friends in the weaving world for generous sharing of thoughts and work for me to hand along to others.

Warm and grateful thanks to my three photographers for their continuing interest and their skill in working with me on the very necessary pictorial part of the book: Beverly Rush, Kent Kammerer, and Harold Tacker.

Very special thanks to Sylvia and Harold Tacker, whose generous giving of time and assistance has enriched this book.

To Nancy Newman, for her interest, encouragement, and support of my writings.

To Diane M. Sugimura, Curator, Costume and Textile Study Center, School of Home Economics, University of Washington, Seattle, my sincere thanks for her interest and time spent helping to provide ethnic material.

My loving thanks to my family, who not only support my weaving and writing efforts, but lovingly help in so many ways. To Sheri, for typing; To Dawn, for prettily posing; To Gary, for expert drawings; and always, to Ron, for his interest and guidance, especially in the exciting space weaving concept.

Jean Wilson

Foreword

This book is the other half of *Weaving You Can Wear*. I planned to have one section of coverings for people, and another section, coverings for places. Each half grew and grew, split at the seam, and became two books. Borrowing the primitive ways of geometric weaving; units; assembling small weavings into larger pieces, or weaving shapes on the loom to fit a need; exploring techniques and the work of present-day weavers—I found that all apply to clothing and household textiles alike. So here in this book are ideas for *you* to borrow. Use them as inspiration when you design and weave fabrics both useful and beautiful.

"Use" is such a small, unassuming word, but it has a vast assortment of meanings. It may seem dull and practical until you begin to equate it with a handcrafted article that has meaning beyond its decorative qualities. Then the word takes on the further connotations: useful; make the most of; utilize; employ; put to work. With these added specific meanings, weaving to use becomes an enjoyable, creative—and useful—occupation.

Introduction

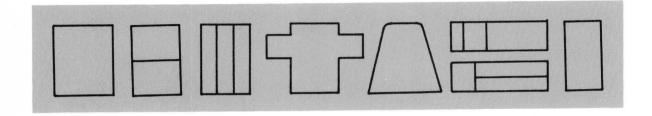

Fashion is a consideration when weaving for your household, but it is not quite so hurried and fleeting as with clothing. Colors and style preferences will determine your choices. Especially if you tend to be fairly conservative, but long to be a bit frivolous, a good general rule is to keep the big, basic things such as carpeting and large pieces of furniture in background colors. Then toss in the flair and daring in smaller, movable, expendable things such as pillows, wall hangings, chair seats, and your own at-home clothes. For a weaver, the clothes can be made from the same yarns and colors as the household weavings. I have done several such commissions, weaving yardage for a hostess gown to blend with the hand-woven upholstery and draperies.

RECTANGLES AND SQUARES
The household textiles selected for this book fit nicely into my format of handwoven rectangles, squares, and combinations—the weaving of small units joined to build a large fabric. The tapestry bedspread, composed of small individual tapestries, is joined by long rectangles of plain weave to make a bed-sized spread. (See Fig. 6-5.) The ethnic wall rug combines squares and rectangles of all sizes into one large rectangular composition. (Fig. 2-3.) Long, narrow table runners are placed on the table, and woven over and under for a covering in true weavers' style! (See ch. 7.)

SHAPED WEAVING
The same principles of shaped weaving that apply to clothing—the loom-shaping of arm-holes, necklines, and so on—are applicable to other weavings. Loom-shaped household fabrics are custom-woven to fit particular needs. For example, a round table could have mats woven in wedge-shaped segments, and a rug, curving outlines to conform to a furniture grouping or to define the walking space. Note the chair pad shaped to the chair in Figure 4-3. These, and more, can be woven to fit the requirements. They are a challenge to the inventiveness of the practical weaver—practical in the sense of useful and right, but *not* dull!

Try some of these ideas:
Weave a chair seat or a loose cushion to perfectly cover an odd-shaped chair.

Weave a wall hanging in several sections to fill a wall space with windows, or to go around a corner, or to hang free as a space-divider between rooms.

Weave a rug in narrow and wider rectangles, to complement a furniture arrangement.

Weave slit-weave tabs at the top of drapery lengths and hang them like a wall hanging.

A headboard for a bed might be a major room feature. Weave it in flat and pile weave. Design and weave the spread to relate, but not dominate.

WOVEN BANDS

Bands fit into the premise of this text. They are units and are usually combined in some way with other bands or weaving. Throughout this book you will find examples of bands used in many ways. Sylvia and Harold Tacker, whose book, *Band Weaving*, is crowded with ways to use bands, had some extra bands for us to play with and with which to try out some of our pet ideas. There were thoughts and applications left over, with no room to show them, such as bands for a room divider, either in a frame or hanging free, or as a flexible door curtain or a semi see-through window screen. Wide bands, stuffed, make braided and woven pillows or coverlets. Bands can be twisted, interwoven, contoured, shaped; worn, hung, and sat upon. The Weaver's Wall is made from Tacker bands (see Fig. 9-1), as are two table textile ideas in chapter 7 (Figs. 7-9 and 7-10) and the pillow covering in Figure 5-10, where bands are used for both warp and weft and woven around the pillow form. (Also, see Sylvia Tacker's stuffed band pillows in ch. 5.)

More uses of bands include tucking wooden spoons in band-holders in your kitchen. I use bands to hold barrettes, hatpins, and other such small items. Tie a bright woven band around your luggage for easy identification. Supplement or repair a basket handle with a sturdy band. Use bands as seam cover-ups or extenders in household textiles and clothing. So hop on the bandwagon and join all the weavers and users of these bright and useful weaving units!

WEAVING SAMPLES

In chapter 7, there is an illustration of a favorite idea—planning and weaving your sampling strips to be used as table textiles or wall composition/reference works. (Fig. 7-2.) If weaving more than one or two identical placemats bores you, too, design and weave the whole set in related colors and patterns. Vary some to keep your interest and craftsmanship in high gear. Weave a planned patch-work quilt, afghan, or baby coverlet. This is a project with great possibilities for correlating colors and patterns.

Looking back at my previous five weaving books, I find that one of my basic beliefs remains unchanged—sample and sample—and make your learning efforts useful. When learning and exploring new techniques, weave a thoughtfully designed sampler/reference as a wall hanging or a pillow cover. Then your design and weaving time will have served a double purpose. Colors and techniques will be visible for reference when you do your next weaving—and not put away out of sight and mind. In learning the twenty-plus ways to achieve a pile surface, my students make a reference/hanging with planned colors and areas for the techniques, using both classic methods and their own adaptations. This piece serves them as a technique reference— to see just how *each* technique looks when woven—as well as reference for yarn use and color combinations.

There is no limit to the ways of creating household weavings. Seeing and solving the problem of providing suitable fabrics for a home, loom-shaping of details or a whole piece of weaving, or joining units into a large textile are exciting prospects and a great challenge to the weaver's expertise and imagination. The more you do, the more ideas occur.

The following chapters contain ideas, methods, and some detailed projects for covering or enhancing floors, walls, windows, tables, beds, and furniture. Some are practical, some fanciful, but, hopefully, all will stimulate your weaving plans. Special projects by groups of weavers and some weavings for children are included.

Every textile technique and pattern has an ethnic source. Just as we draw on uses and styles of clothing, we turn to historical weavings for inspiration and guidance for our modern household weavings. This brings us to chapter 1 on ethnic weavings.

Chapter 1

Ethnic Weavings and Their Uses

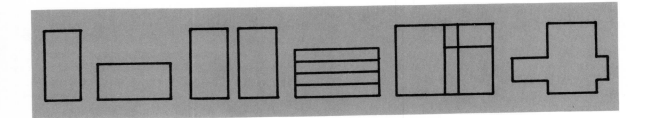

Weaving You Can Wear presented clothing based upon and adapted from primitive methods of weaving geometric shapes and shaping garments on the loom. Household weavings assembled from small woven units also have precedents. Early weavings were functional. Even textiles which seem just decorative to us, and those we use in a decorative way, had a real use and reason for being. While weavers and all craftsmen now are of today and it behooves us to look to the future and explore new ways to use new fibers, still the roots of our craft go back to the first textile fabrications and uses. There is so much to be learned by studying methods and uses of color and design. We can extract what we need from early and ethnic weavings, then use this heritage to weave for our day and needs. Making large weavings out of many small ones is not news—weavers have always made textiles on small looms and simply added them together for the size required. In the past:

Sleeping mats were woven and pieced together.

Housewives wove linen sheets and joined the strips with fine seams.

Mats for wind-screens were woven and hung in tropical homes.

Tapestries and thick rugs were hung on walls more for insulation than decoration.

In long, cold Scandinavian winters, deep pile rugs were used as bed covers.

Endlessly useful, bands were woven in widths from about an inch to a foot or more. Fifteen-inch bands served as baby wrappers to hold baby on mother's back. Narrow forehead bands held heavy loads on backs and heads.

SOURCES OF DESIGN AND USE

Regional and cultural patterns, methods, colors, and yarns are sources of inspiration for weavers of today. A tiny pattern may be the start of an important, large-scale design. The stylized pattern centering Lila Winn's handsome pillow (see Fig. 5-16) came from Montezuma's personal emblem. She adapted and wove it as one large medallion.

Figure 1-2 is a detail of the intricate pattern of a very old rug in fine soumak technique. Figure 1-1 shows the whole small rug. The colors—two rich blues, natural off-white, and warm orange-red—are mellowed with age and use. Studying a rug like this under a magnifying glass is informative. It is fascinating to see just how the weaver adapted the soumak technique to the design and color changes. Subtle differences in texture occur where soumak countered rows are combined with those woven all in one direction, in and around a pattern. Much can be learned by exploring the methods, motifs, and color handling in just one rug.

Notice the way Turkish saddle bags are joined with an ingenious looping of wool cords and can easily be laid flat as a rug or cover.

When we call a throw a nap-robe, or a small coverlet an "afghan," we are probably indebted to an ethnic source for the name and/or the idea for these most comforting weavings. Not of an overwhelming size and made of soft and cuddly yarns, they are great favorites with weavers. They can be wildly colored or restful and quiet. (See Fig. 6-20.)

A two-fisted potholder from Ireland may not exactly be an ethnic idea, but it is a useful and practical item from another country. The one we purchased was of heavy white cotton string, very tightly woven. You could make some as colorful as an Irish rainbow! Weave a long rectangle of heavy cotton, about 6 in. wide and 42 in. long. Fold each end up to make a pocket, about 7 in. deep, sewing along the sides. If your material is not very heavy, you may need to find it twice, so allow for that in the length. You end up with a very handy double-pocket holder for taking hot dishes out of the oven with both hands. You will require at least twelve inches between pockets —more if your pans are huge.

You may not have a sledge seat to cover warmly with a rya rug as in old Finland, but you might fling your newly woven rug into a modern molded chair!

You will not need a Chilkat ceremonial blanket to wear, but the design idea is there for a wall hanging. (See Figs. 3-6 and 3-7.)

Fig. 1-1. The whole soumak weave rug, showing division of space and wide borders. Courtesy Mr. and Mrs. Harold Tacker. (Photographs of Figs. 1-1 and 1-2 by Harold Tacker)

Fig. 1-2. Medallion detail of soumak weave rug. (Also see color section, C-2.)

ASSEMBLED WOVEN STRIPS

Figure 1-3 illustrates a wide Indonesian textile assembled from three strips. The 7 in.-wide cream-white center, with a small laid-in medallion, is joined to two side strips 18 in. wide. These strips have warp-patterned stripes in dark blue and off-white on a ground of mellowed orange-red. Study and learn from the well-balanced placement of both plain and patterned stripes. The strips are neatly sewn.

Where the weaving just stops at each end, the very fine, crisp cotton warp twists into fringes. The whole weaving is about 43 in. × 80 in., so it was presumably meant for a bed cover. It would do as well for a wall hanging or a table cover. Weavers of the Tuareg group in West Africa make heavy tapestry-weave blankets of camel's hair or sometimes of sheep's wool. As with other West African cloth, the blankets are of narrow strips, with patterned and plain strips joined together. In weight, they are unlike the fine-cotton country cloth strips used for clothing. The blankets are soft of surface, but quite compact and firm. Usually woven in natural white, browns, and blacks, the patterns are small and geometric, much like the African print designs. A fine blanket I saw looked almost quilted, because the tapestry weave patterns were tightly woven against the much looser plain areas. There is an idea to try! The blanket in Figure 1-4 is assembled and sewn with strips that are not exactly lined up to match in the joining. The interesting result is a slightly wavering pattern—as if you were viewing it through water, which gives another design idea to work with!

A NOTE OF INTEREST

A total environment is assembled from narrow handwoven strips by the nomadic Tuareg people of West Africa. The cloth is cotton with elaborate patterns woven in. Strips are sewn together into a voluminous fabric, which is used for the sides of a large tent. The roof is made of leather. To provide ventilation and a bit of light, the strips are left unsewed for a few inches at intervals. The textile is practical for people on the move, it can be folded flat, and is much more handsome than plain canvas!

You may want to design and weave a blanket (or tent) in similar fashion. Spin and weave natural sheep's wool, or perhaps try some of the more exotic fibers and yarns that are now becoming available. The rapidly growing interest in spinning, and weaving with hand-spun yarns, has stimulated the market for rare and beautiful fibers such as camel's hair, cashmere, llama, and many varieties and colors of sheep's wool and goat hair. Look at the advertisements in *Shuttle, Spindle and Dyepot* magazine for sources of unspun and hand-spun fibers such as silk, wools, and cotton.

Here is a yardage challenge: The Mossi weavers of Upper Volta and Northern Ghana prepare their long, narrow woven strips for market by rolling more than 400 yards round and round into huge wheels!

Another use for woven strips: You might adapt a woven border idea from the weavers of Bokhara, Turcoman, and Khiva rugs who put borders, about 6 in. × 10 ft., with plain weave ground and rug patterns woven in cut pile, around tent walls, like a molding, where the sides meet the roof. Borders like this might be applied to a wall as a frame for small weavings or a tapestry.

Fig. 1-4. This Tuareg camel's hair blanket was woven in narrow strips in black, white, yellow, and brown-red. From ''Introducing West African Cloth,'' by Kate P. Kent, reprinted with permission of the author and Denver Museum of Natural History.

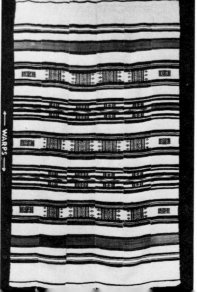

Fig. 1-3. Indonesian textile, made of three sections joined. Courtesy of Elizabeth Raleigh. (Photograph by Harold Tacker)

SHAPED AND ARRANGED WEAVINGS

Shaped household weavings do not seem to be very prevalent, generally, but rectangles and squares of different sizes were often combined to fill a given space.

Turkish carpets made especially for use at court were in the shape of a cross, to cover a table. You can borrow this idea for a table or a bedspread, to eliminate those bulky corners in a heavy fabric. Some camel-trappings were shaped or made up from combinations of narrow and wide rugs.

The traditional carpet plan in a Persian home was composed of three sizes of carpets, placed in specific relationships: two long, narrow rectangles and two wider ones, of different lengths.

The Japanese tatami mats are woven to a standard size, so a room is a 6-mat, or an 8-mat room, for instance.

TATAMI MAT ARRANGEMENTS

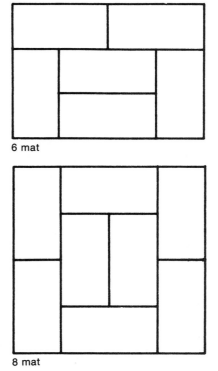

6 mat

8 mat

RUGS AND CARPETS

Floor coverings are perhaps the most commonly used and widely known ethnic weavings. Oriental rugs—kilim, soumak, and cut-pile Ghiordes knot—are long-wearing and beautiful, and usually put to practical use. Chinese, Navaho, Scandinavian, Moroccan, American rag carpets; flat weave rugs from India; sea grass, hemp, and other natural fibers woven into strips, squares, or mats—each one is distinctive in concept and technique and all serve to cover floors handsomely, adding comfort and richness to rooms.

Saddlebags in carpet weaves are perfect for large floor pillows, as are small rugs, blending floor coverings and pillows into a comfortable, relaxing environment.

This is pure conjecture, but I like to think that maybe woven floor-coverings originated in the following way. In large, drafty stone castle halls, tapestries were hung across doorways and window apertures. Fur pelts were on the beds, and reeds and straw were strewn on the floor for a kind of cover. One day, as she waited for her man to return from the current crusade, a lady of one of these castles had had enough, and more, of the slippery, sliding grasses. She idly picked up a few and began interlacing them. Soon she became quite pleased with the nice flat mat she was creating, and sent hand-maidens out to gather long cattail leaves. She plaited and wove and soon had neat floor coverings. Later, she cut worn hides into strips and wove them in, too, as well as strips from old clothing. So—neat, warm, flat floor coverings were created and enjoyed. Warm underfoot, and warming to see.

Carpets had great significance in court life and churches. They gave visible indications of the boundary lines between the exalted and the common people—a separation defined by custom, rules, and actual carpeted areas.

Richly patterned, valued carpets were put up on tables as well as floors, steps, and balcony railings.

Carpets in use—and, more importantly, carpet designs—were meticulously painted into portraits and frescoes as early as 1200. Some patterns and colors would have been lost except for these art works. In the fifteenth century, Holbein the Younger reproduced a certain type of geometric patterned carpet so often that those carpets became known as "Holbein" carpets. He often showed them as table covers—no doubt at the request of the prideful owner being portrayed with and in his finery.

HANGINGS

We no longer need to hang large tapestries in vast rooms to cut the drafts, but we can and do make wall hangings to suit our more modest dwellings and to enhance public buildings. Some tapestries were hung in folds from large hooks in stone walls. This idea can be translated into a tapestry weaving designed to be hung in this way, as a departure from a flat tapestry. The more delicate ethnic weavings such as runners, large cloths, valances, are most often displayed on a wall and enjoyed as a pictorial textile.

TEXTILE USES IN OTHER COUNTRIES

Living as we do in our household-textile world, it comes as a surprise to find comparatively few household cloths in some parts of the world. In a study of domestic textiles of other places and how they are used, we have found some interesting comparisons. There seem to be fewer specific household fabrics than we are accustomed to. In some cultures, dower chests bulge with lovingly crafted bed linens, towels, bed coverings, hangings, and the like, but in others, a large square or rectangle, woven in strips and joined or woven on a wide loom, is used interchangeably as a bed cover, a table cover, or a shawl. When there are fewer possessions, each item does double or triple duty. Maybe we should take heed and consider more than one way to use our handwovens, too.

All of the following, which are in the collection of the Costume and Textile Study Center, Home Economics Department, University of Washington, Seattle, are representative of the types of domestic fabrics woven and were chosen for their design and use, as suggestions.

The extensive collection from India yielded the following household textiles: Figure 1-5 is a detail of a Hindu *durrie*—a flat weave rug woven in plain weave tapestry techniques with dovetail, hatching, and slanted color-change joinings. A very stylized peacock and patterned borders are woven in grayed greens, reds, white, and yellow.

A pictorial curtain panel from Orissa state is shown in Figure 1-6. All colors are used to weave a temple with animals, birds, and pennants. The bands across the bottom and up the sides are of a typical Indian pattern. We would probably call this a wall hanging and use it as such.

The next three items have multiple uses and may provide some pattern inspiration, too. The fine cotton textile from Andhia Pradesh in Figure 1-7 can be used either as a bedspread or as a curtain. Rows of black patterns, including pairs of birds, are inlaid on a yellow ground.

A bed sheet—or a tea cloth! The fine cotton in Figure 1-8 has a neat plaidlike pattern of o's and x's. The colors are dark blue on a medium blue background and a single white thread defines the pattern lines.

Bedspread—or a man's shawl! From Punjab States, District Karmal, Figure 1-9 has a woven all-over pattern in nearly every color, with large medallions in a regular repeat in the center. The wide border of three patterns is repeated in bands. Very fine stripes make up the edge border and section divisions.

So it is clear that the large rectangles serve in unexpected ways.

Fig. 1-5. A flat weave rug in tapestry technique from India. Figures 1-5 to 1-15 are all courtesy of the Costume and Textile Study Center, School of Home Economics, University of Washington. (Photographs by William Eng)

Fig. 1-6. Note the infinite, fine details in the domes and roofs of this curtain panel.

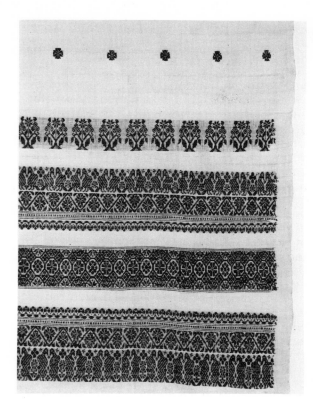

Fig. 1-7. Black design on yellow ground for a textile that can be used as a bedspread—or as a curtain.

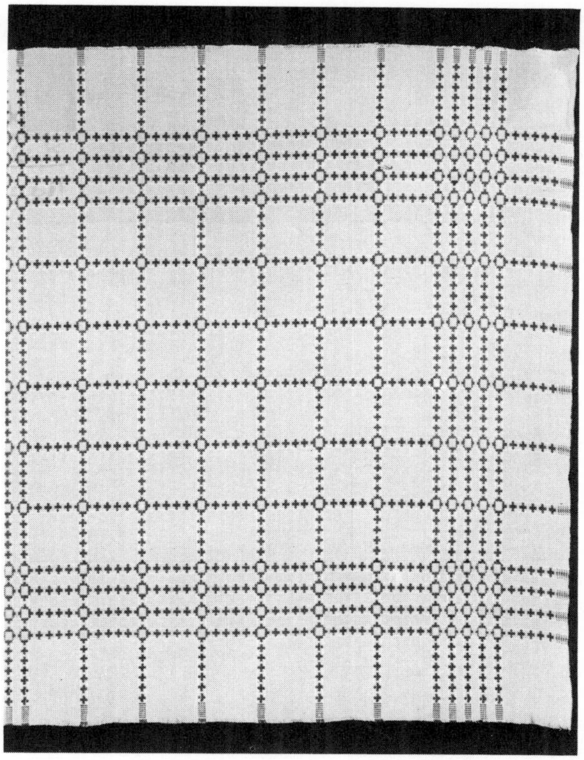

Fig. 1-8. Double use: as a bed sheet or a tea cloth.

Fig. 1-9. Used for a bedspread or a man's shawl. Note the interesting use of large and small patterns with stripes.

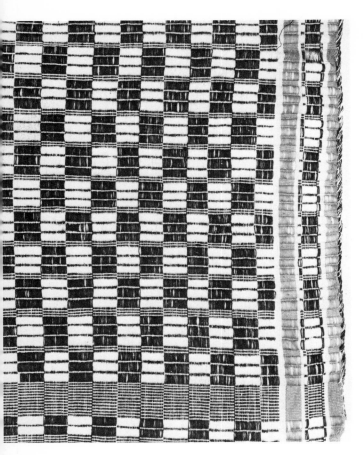

Exceptionally heavy white weft is woven across a fine black, white, and yellow warp in a design of narrow rectangles, to make the quilt in Figure 1-10. The selvedge is finished with a black-and-white twisted cord.

Figure 1-11 shows a thickly padded blue-and-white quilt from Gujarat state, Broach. It is double weave, plumped up with wadding which is put in between the two layers of fabric during the weaving. Note the basically simple pattern of rectangles, stripes, and checkerboard at the corner, and how it looks more complex when you offset the stripes of dark and light.

The bathtowel in Figure 1-12 and washcloth in Figure 1-13 have a looped "Turkish towel" or terry-cloth surface. Colors reverse in the identical pattern on the other side. These items would look in place in a store today. The towel has a geometric tan, white, and blue pattern woven on a ground of brown, yellow, and red, with a wide border of flat weave. The washcloth is more subdued, with an overall pattern of white on green. The fringe on each is secured with a simple hemstitch. Figure 1-14 shows a colorful hand towel from Kerala state. Of a very fine cotton, it is woven in a loom pattern of yellow and red diamonds, and has dark red deer on a yellow ground lined up along the border. The hem is hand hemstitched.

Fig. 1-10. A black, white, and yellow quilt with thick weft and very fine warp.

Fig. 1-11. A padded double-weave quilt in blue and white.

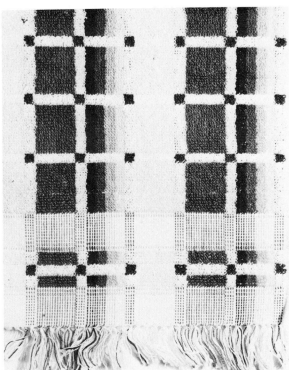

Fig. 1-12. Bath towel with flat weave and terry-cloth loops.

22

Do you have any use for a saddlebag? It's not usually a household textile, but the one in Figure 1-15 has deep pockets and is a good model for the play-pocket mentioned in chapter 8. A length of heavy closely woven cotton with a wide-patterned border was simply turned back up to make the pocket. A tassel is sewn to each corner. You could adapt this idea to a number of uses, from an apron with deep pockets to a hanging-holder for dried weeds (Fig. 1-16), small household clutter, toys, or what you will—or perhaps, just as a hanging to look at. The interesting pattern in Figure 1-15 appears to be figures holding hands, alternating headstands. About 14 in. × 21 in. with 10 in. pockets, the saddlebag is of natural cotton, with a red, green, yellow, and purple pattern.

Fig. 1-15. Saddle bag of unbleached cotton with multicolored pattern on the deep pocket.

Fig. 1-13. Washcloth of white and green terry-cloth.

Fig. 1-14. Hand towel with an overall diamond pattern and a red border on the yellow ground.

Fig. 1-16. A weed pocket with warp fringes. (Photograph by Harold Tacker)

23

Fig. 1-17. Calabrian inlay pillow top from Italy.

Fig. 1-18. Detail of the bird in the Calabrian pillow. The surface turns of the inlaid pattern make a strong outline. Flowers are in pile weave.

Some other articles from the textile study center which are not pictured include some curtains made of panels of cotton, with small scattered motifs woven in, and patterned borders, much like the *sari* fabrics in design but of heavier weight. One curtain has ikat bands and rows of inlay, yellow on light blue.

Some of the tablecloths have a fringe and ball edging added, while others are finished with a simple warp fringe.

Among the items from Italy is a pillow top with borders and birds, woven in the distinctive Calabrian inlay technique, with some looped pile. This pillow is a good example of how the surface turn of the laid-in pattern weft defines the outline of the design unit. Figure 1-17 shows half of the pillow and the detail in Figure 1-18 shows the technique.

In many countries, housewives find numerous and essential uses in and outside the home for squares of firmly woven cloth. They act as carryalls, food and basket covers, baby-carriers, or for whatever other use can be made of them. The utility cloths of Mexico and Guatemala have their counterpart in the *furoshiki* of Japan; an enveloping Irish wool shawl holds a tinker's baby close along with parcels, or a cotton kerchief carries a few new-laid eggs into a farm kitchen. Often these cloths are beautifully handcrafted with printed or handwoven patterns belying their utilitarian purpose.

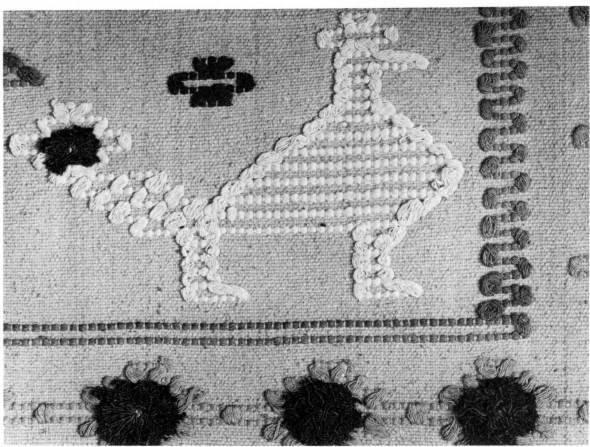

Serviettas: The indispensable and picturesque cotton cloths of Mexico might be as small as a palm, to hold under a ceremonial drinking gourd, or a large rectangle to cover a family altar. Of cotton, with bright woven patterns freely expressed, these weavings are not rigidly held to symbolic motifs. Worn as a head cloth, or bearing candles to church or tortillas for a journey, they are useful individually designed textiles.

The *Tzutes* of Guatemala are usually larger than the Mexican cloths, but serve much the same purposes and are also woven in bright cottons. They may be a yard square and are made from two narrow widths of material. Often small patterns are scattered in a mix of brilliant color or perhaps just one color is woven on a white ground. Since this woven article is not as tied to symbolic tradition as are other parts of a Guatemalan costume, some of the brocade weave patterns display humor and whimsy. When part of the costume, it is worn as a shawl or folded for a head covering, but is also put to work as a food cover or baby carrier.

Furoshiki: The utility cloths of Japan are squares of cotton or silk, colorfully printed in floral or geometric patterns. They, too, have many uses, and one of the most charming is that of presenting gifts wrapped in a lovely square of cloth.

We could very well adopt this custom of weaving beautiful squares of fabric for carryalls and extend their use to table textiles, pillow covers, or small shawls. I find them easy and suitable for transporting lunches, small shopping packages, or to tuck into a suitcase for a small evening bag, as a refreshing change from a handbag or basket. A more complex woven carrier is the all-purpose weaver's bag which is assembled from one very long and one short and wide rectangle. (See pp. 118–119 for the weaving plan of this article and a baby-carrier version in Fig. 8-10.)

Two Guatemalan *tzutes* in Figures 1-19 and 1-20 are long-time favorites of mine for different reasons. The hand-woven white cotton one is embroidered with red-and-yellow dots—and an occasional lavender one. Unexpected, simple yet sophisticated, it seems quite atypical. The pattern is embroidered rather than woven in, but it is presented as a design idea.

The amusing woven-in pattern in Figure 1-20 includes bicycle riders wheeling across in two rows—on square wheels! Another section has animals, trees, and birds, along with conventional fine stripes and bands of stylized leaf and flower patterns. Both *tzutes* are in the extensive Arthur Loveless collection of Guatemalan textiles presented to the Textile and Costume Study Center by the Seattle Weavers' Guild.

If we follow the same design- and use-philosophy as that of the long-ago weavers and craftsmen who made their daily work tools beautiful with carvings and decorations—wove baskets and cases for storing and using or carefully made mats and coverings—then it is also valid for us to make needle cases and shuttle holders; potholders, purses, place mats, and pads; carry-alls and all manner of large and small coverings. We are weaving for our esthetic and practical needs, as they did.

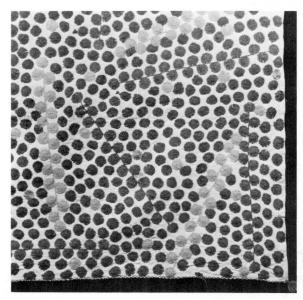

Fig. 1-19. The detail of a Guatemalan *tzute* shows circles which were embroidered in many-stranded fine cotton, in an eye stitch, on handwoven cotton.

Fig. 1-20. *Tzute* with wide pattern bands and fine stripes. Note the square wheels on the bikes!

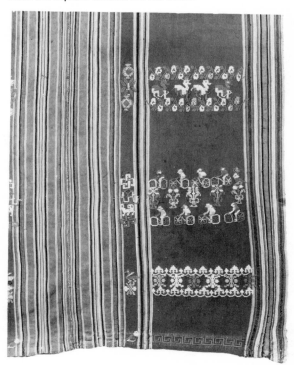

Chapter 2

Floor Coverings

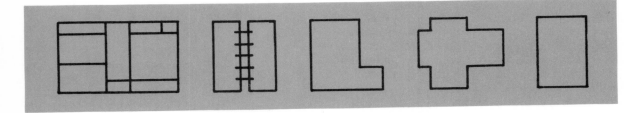

Rugs run the gamut from bright, bold accents of color and pattern, through more subdued and subtle patterns and colors, to the always harmonious natural wool colors of brown, white, and black. A good rug design will allow the rug to stay on the floor, visually. Unless it is the one important accent in the room, an area rug should be designed to be a part of the whole scheme of furniture, major floor areas, walls, and not leap up at you. An intrusive rug design is one that makes you walk around the rug rather than upon it. If a rug becomes so important because of color and pattern, it might be best to hang it on the wall to look at instead of placing it on the floor. This is what happened to the Ethnic Wall Rug and the reason it was used as a wall decoration. (Details of that project will follow on the next page.) Both quiet and "busy" rugs will be shown.

Originally, some of the richly piled Scandinavian rugs were used on walls for protection from the bitter cold of the long winters. So there is a real precedent for hanging a heavy rug as a decorative wall piece.

When you plan a floor covering, consider what will be placed on and around it. If everything is patterned and colorful and highly textured, nothing will really be seen and appreciated, and some of your weaving effort will be lost. A madly busy rug is distracting when you read, rest, or wish to have quiet conversations. A small area may need a daring spot of color, but this might better be a floor cushion, or several bright pillows, which are more easily moved about than a floor covering. Figure 2-1 is an example of what I think of as a quiet rug. It is woven in four shades of gray-green to dull gold in Greek soumak, with very large rug wool and Persian rug yarns. Its impact derives from the rich texture and subdued colors creating a background. However, I don't mean to imply that *all* floor covering must be dull, understated, and go unnoticed. Just apply good design and color principles and have your handwoven rug or carpet the right color and pattern for the surroundings and use. Think of the total effect when you plan to cover a floor.

Fig. 2-1. A detail of a "quiet" rug woven in Greek soumak in muted colors. Woven by author.

JOINING RUG UNITS

Units woven in different techniques can be joined with colors and joinings planned for harmonious effect. Some parts can be flat weave—some can have a raised surface of loops or cut pile. The joining itself can be a major design element and the main interest in a flat-weave rug. Tied wefts, five-strand joining, Sorbello stitch are all suitable for joining, which can be made important by using large-sized wools, contrasting colors, and expanding the stitches to large scale.

Fill floor space with units, woven to be interchanged for total shape and design variety. For instance, seven squares and a rectangle can be shifted around into several different shapes and patterns. If the grouping is not right, just subtract from, add to it, or change it about.

ETHNIC WALL RUG

After a long time writing about weaving rugs in units designed to be joined, I followed my own advice, combining rectangles and squares together in a planned rug design. This plan and a desire to weave ethnic patterns culminated in a rug in which each unit was a different size, woven on frame looms. (Fig. 2-2.)

Fig. 2-2. One unit of the Ethnic Wall Rug in progress on the canvas stretcher frame loom. All sections were made on frame looms of different sizes.

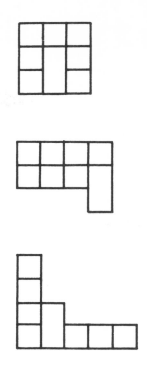

SEVEN SQUARES
AND A RECTANGLE

My weaving, designing, and writing about textiles have always reflected a deep interest and pleasure in the continuing study of older cultures and crafts and ethnic patterns, colors, and techniques—an interest exemplified by the Ethnic Wall Rug. This is a real rug, woven in rug techniques with heavy wool rug yarns from Greece, Mexico, and Sweden. Since it is also pictorial and decorative, it has been put on the wall—at least to start with. (Figs. 2-3 to 2-6 and C-1 in the color section.)

The rug's fourteen units reflect the influence of these ethnic sources freely translated: Oriental rugs, Sweden, Northwest Indian, Mexico, Europe, Peru, Ireland, Egyptian Coptic. An additional influence on the whole composition of this eclectic collection are Piet Mondrian paintings!

Techniques for the rug included Ghiordes Knot, both cut and left in loops; Oriental and single soumak; plain weave tapestry; and one unit with a background of the Bayeux tapestry needlework laid technique. The rich, muted colors of Oriental rugs influenced color choices.

Fig. 2-3. The Ethnic Wall Rug comprises fourteen units, woven independently and joined in a composition. (See also Figure C-1 in the color section.)

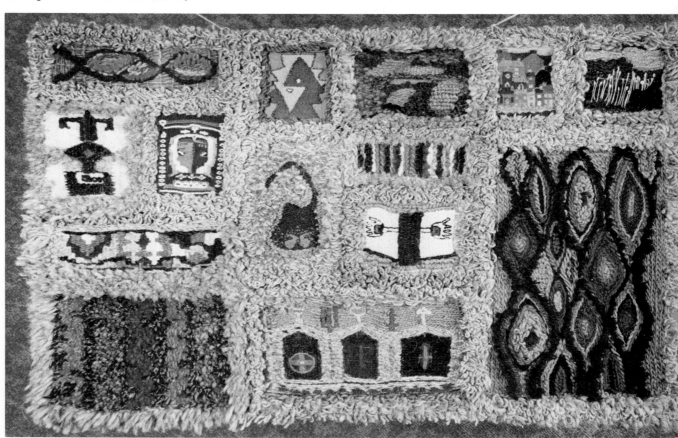

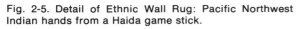

Fig. 2-4. Detail of Ethnic Wall Rug showing classic Peruvian fish motif, framed with one row of green rug wool-loops and the border of gray goat-hair yarn.

Fig. 2-6. Detail of Ethnic Wall Rug shows influence of Mexican flat stamp patterns. Figures 2-3 to 2-6 all woven by author. (Photographs by Kent Kammerer)

Fig. 2-5. Detail of Ethnic Wall Rug: Pacific Northwest Indian hands from a Haida game stick.

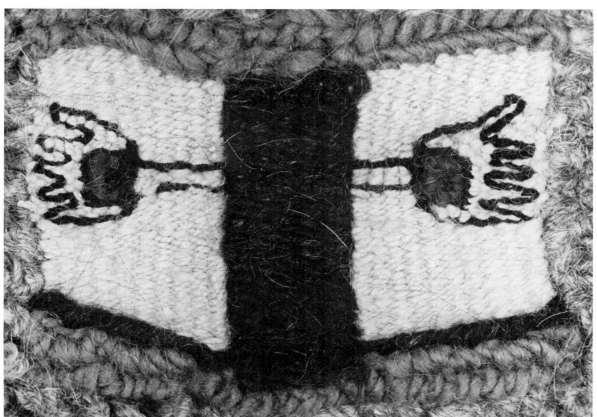

A common denominator unifying the whole is the border of coarse, wiry Greek goat-hair yarn in raised loops and cut pile. The patterns are woven with Persian and Swedish rug wools and colored Greek goat-hair yarns. The gray handspun yarn is lively, with a slightly uneven handspun look, and should wear forever. All colors are somewhat muted, because, as mentioned, the intention was to achieve some of the mellowed look of used and treasured Oriental rugs.

The composition plan was that of units and borders placed to emphasize design lines, and to balance the colors and sizes of the units. A remarkable thing happened after I had made the basic plans and begun weaving. An issue of *National Geographic* arrived in the mail with a double-page photograph of newly washed Persian rugs drying on a bumpy gray hillside near Tehran, Iran. Here was my project before me—gray borders, muted rug colors, varied sizes and all!

Each separate unit suggested its own technique and colors. Most weaving methods were chosen to express the particular source of the design. For example, rya technique was used for the Scandinavian unit and plain weave tapestry for the Coptic portrait.

As when you make a sampling file, a project like this becomes a reminder of various design sources and a color reference. The unit and design idea could be used very well in lighter types of weaving, and put together for a bedspread, wall hanging, or a screen. This same general idea might be a good one using single motifs from Oriental rugs, medallions, mandalas, Persian miniature details; parts of ornate illuminated pages of the Book of Kells or Book of Durrow; Indian patterns, ancient mosaics, and so on. Isolate, abstract, simplify, and make your own weavable designs. Plan narrow or important joinings. With a raised surface, such as loops, the joining itself will be hidden. Plan a flat hand-stitched joining, with flat woven borders on each unit.

Whatever your source, do plan an overall composition so the result will be designed and orderly. Avoid hit-and-miss confusion. Relate all units in color and techniques, so that the same ones occur in each section but change with the subject.

For a neater assemblage that is easier to put together, be careful about *even* borders, straight edges, and careful measurements to fit the plan. Design lines that follow through to set the pattern should be emphasized.

Some of the small tapestries in the Ethnic Wall Rug were used before, but I planned to include them in one composition and it turned out to be this one. The three little thumbnail sketch tapestries done in Ireland, the Peruvian Fish motif, and the Coptic-style Janus heads fit into the theme of this rug and so were given the gray goat-hair borders and included.

Although I made a sketch of the proposed arrangement and designs at the start, the finished rug varies somewhat from the plan. Putting the rug together, finally, was like assembling a big jigsaw puzzle; shifting units until sizes, patterns, and colors seemed right. The final result is quite similar to the original composition, even though some units are different than had been planned. This is quite understandable since the entire project—the designing and weaving—was in progress for more than a year. The overall piece was adjusted in size also. The original plan was for at least two more rows of units, but since it was becoming quite heavy and the proportions seemed to balance out, it was ended as shown. There are enough unit designs to make another rug!

FINISHING THE ETHNIC WALL RUG

To stabilize each unit and give further strength when it is used as a rug or hung on the wall, the back of the rug was lined with a firmly woven gray cotton homespun cloth. When it is put on the floor, a thin foam rubber pad will be placed under it. I didn't use burlap, because of its self-destruct qualities of rotting out. Some precautions had to be taken to avoid sagging and bulging in the wrong places. Because of the weight, each unit was quilted to the backing with strong gray linen thread, in the manner of tying a quilt. Some areas required more stitches than others. For more textural interest, some areas were slightly padded—some of the ogee shapes, the Irish fields, and the Janus heads for example. The flat tapestries were fastened at a few points inside the borders so they would be flat and framed by the deep pile surrounding them. With one selvedge along the bottom, the 60 in. cloth left about 12 in. at the top for a folded tube hem. A 1 in. × 2 in. length of wood was inserted for the full width to serve as a sturdy hanger. Two heavy screw eyes put in toward the center allow hanging on wall hooks. The hardware is nearly hidden in the deep border, and the wood is hidden in the hem.

The unit in the upper left corner is the only nonwoven section. Because I wanted to include some of the Bayeux tapestry laid technique, I did this small area on rug canvas with a needle, using Ghiordes knots and Oriental soumak, as well.

The Ethnic Wall Rug provided some lessons which I learned and noted for a "next time." The hours and hours spent were a mix of joy, frustration, a deep draw on experience, and a lot of satisfaction in the planning and the doing. The rug is just about the size limit to handle easily. It is very heavy, and another row would have made it awkward to cope with and a problem to hang. Next time, I would make the borders more uniformly even. In this composition, the planned casualness of some borders just looked like poor design instead of the unstudied look of the rugs on the hillside. That unstudied effect might be best in a tapestry. To even up the major design lines—the heavy ones—I added some extra rows of gray pile with a needle, weaving in where needed.

The diagram on this page is a numbered plan of the Ethnic Wall Rug and shows the strong design lines of the composition. The units and their design sources:

1. Bayeux Tapestry laid technique, which is something like couching, where strands of yarn are laid on the ground fabric and sewn down with an overcast stitch. The catch stitches are evenly spaced, forming a subtle pattern. Ghiordes knot and Oriental soumak techniques make the central pattern.

2. Plain weave tapestry with a motif similar to those in Mexican flat stamps of baked clay.

3. Coptic-style heads in plain weave tapestry.

4. Kelim (slit weave) technique in a geometric pattern typical of those found in Kelim rugs.

5. Scandinavian influence in the pattern, colors, and use of several strands of different wools in each Ghiordes knot.

6. Communal Prayer Rug. Intrigued with the various Oriental rug styles, I was delighted at the idea of a communal prayer rug. Private prayer space for several persons, all in one long rug, seems like a practical and sociable custom. So a miniature of one was woven.

7. Pacific Northwest Indian. The fascination of hands as they appear in carvings and paintings by long-ago Northwest Indian craftsmen inspired the motif in this unit. Similar outflung hands are on one of a large set of Indian gambling sticks.

8. *Mir-i-bota* or *Bhuta* are just two names given to the hooked pattern that appears frequently in Persian and Indian rugs and paisley patterns. The image has many meanings—such as print of a closed fist, flames, meandering riverbeds, among others —but it looks rather like a crook-neck squash!

9. Stripes as seen in some middle-European handwoven skirts and aprons.

10. Peruvian stylized double-fish pattern.

11. The patchwork pattern of fields and hedgerows.

12. Irish houses.

13. River reeds.

14. Ogee pattern found in many cultures in many techniques and media—prints, carvings, and weavings.

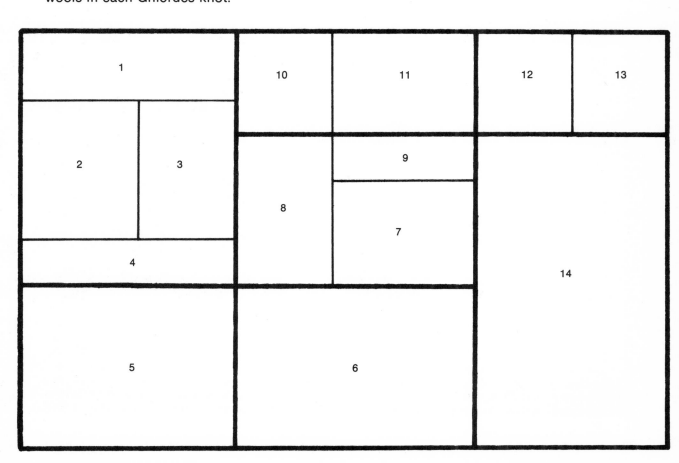

A TIED JOINING

A joining can be a simple seam hidden in a surface texture, it can be made important by a special selvedge treatment and needlework joining stitches, or it can be accomplished on the loom during the weaving to become the main design feature.

A tied joining has many applications. Examples, suggestions, procedures, and variations are given, and you will discover others.

Tied wefts were used as a color-change joining in a rug woven in Oriental soumak in Figure 2-7. One row of tabby was inserted between soumak rows, with the soumak always starting at the left, thus slanting in the same direction throughout. In the hairy rug yarn, a single tie holds when the rows are beaten in tightly. The slant of the tie repeats the slant of the soumak.

In an example for demonstration purposes (Fig. 2-8), two versions of the knot are shown. The first four from the bottom are double knotted, with the yarn twisted and pulled to fall on the opposite-color side. The next four are single ties, as in the rug detail in Figure 2-7, and the colors fall on opposite sides without twisting.

Fig. 2-7. Tied wefts were used as a joining at the color-change point on a soumak weave rug.

WEAVING THE WEFT TIE

In a raised surface or soumak weave with tabby rows alternating, the ties can be made with tabby ends or pattern weft ends, or both, depending upon how close you want the knot-loops.

Loops should not be so long that they become heel-catchers.

Tie one or two at the start to see what length the ties should be, and how much weft to extend. In our example, using heavy rug wool, the loops were about 2 in. long. The light yarn is a single strand; the dark, which is somewhat finer, is used doubled.

Bring the loop out under the warp on each side for a smoother single tie.

Always tie in the same direction for a more precise line of bows, but tie the opposite direction or at random for a casual look. We put light over dark each time. The real beauty of this join is in the repeated precision of the loops and the center line of the knots.

Use your judgment about single or double tie. Some yarns will readily twist to the contrast side—some won't. The single tie is secure when the yarn is clingy and weaving rows well packed in.

Weave and tie each row, or weave several rows on either side, then join several. Adjustments can be made in tightening and straightening the loops when the row is all woven.

If the line of knots gets too thick and bulky, interloop several rows of weft, then tie the wefts only every third or fourth row. The need for this will be obvious and will depend upon your warp sett (number of warps per inch) and the size of the weft yarn.

VARIATIONS ON WEFT TIE WEAVING

When you are weaving and joining at the same time, move the color blocks about in a pattern, as we did in Figure 2-7.

Use a third color for the tabby and join those rows for loops that contrast with both sides. Or use a different-colored tabby in each side with two or more colors in the body of the rug for an intricate color distribution.

This joining will work as well with cut ends, or with cut and looped ends combined.

On one side of the join, the surface can be looped or cut pile—on the other side, a plain or other flat weave, with ties matching or contrasting.

OTHER USES OF THE WEFT TIE

This same weft tie can be used as a joining of units, planned and woven with extended wefts. Weave a "sloppy" selvedge, with wefts out in loops along the edge. Two pieces are joined by knotting the loops together, as just described. If you are joining several units, side by side, the wefts will have to be extended on both sides of the weaving. If they are edge sections, one side will be a conventional selvedge. This join is most effective when two colors are used, but can be used other ways, too. It is a good way to join strips of a blanket or throw; for clothing seams where the small bows would be the trim; or in large or small-scale hangings, dividers, or pillows.

Fig. 2-8. Two ways to do the tied weft knot for a joining of units. The bottom four are double knot, the top four single overhand knot. Figures 2-7 and 2-8 woven by author. (Photographs by Harold Tacker)

HIDDEN JOINING

A small fluffy rug woven by Harold Tacker is an example of a rug woven in strips and joined invisibly. (Fig. 2-9.) It was woven on a narrow loom in two strips, with Ghiordes knots and several strands and colors in each knotting weft. The meandering casual pattern of color change in the deep and shaggy rug disguises the joining down the center. Best results are achieved with this random changing of color when you have at least a general idea of where the colors will repeat and carry over in an intriguing way. The pillow shown with the rug was woven and joined in the same way, but with slightly different colors.

ONE-PIECE RUGS

Rugs are probably most often woven in one piece, with the dimensions limited by the loom width and capacity. A sturdy loom is required for weaving large heavy rugs, but lighter-weight rugs are satisfactorily produced on frame, backstrap, vertical, or floor looms. Do suit the scale of size and yarns to the loom for a successful result.

Fig. 2-9. Pile rug woven in two long rectangles and joined invisibly. Weaver, Harold Tacker. (Photograph by Harold Tacker)

From the infinite variety of rug-weaving methods, only five examples were selected. Each one of these rugs represents a particular weaving procedure: double weave, a loom-controlled weave which results in a rug with a comfortable padded feel from the two interlaced layers of weaving; hand-knotted cut pile for a sumptuous surface; flat weave, showing yarns and woven patterns to good advantage; an 8-harness weave with the colors reversed on opposite sides; woven pile on both sides of a reversible rug. Beyond these are other techniques and many variations, so the choice is wide and challenging when you plan a way to weave a floor covering.

Lila Winn wove an award-winning rug of natural white, black, and gray handspun wool in double weave on a gray linen warp (Fig. 2-10). The reversible double weave in heavy wool provides a pleasant, resilient padded feeling and adds richness to the texture of the plain weave. Note the detail of plaited fringe at the edge in Figure 2-11. The two rows of long and full fringe complete the overall design. The gray linen fringe is the warp. Black wool was added in with a needle, then plaited and finished with stubby ends shorter than the alternating gray fringe, thus repeating the effect of the rectangles in the body of the rug.

Fig. 2-10. Double weave handspun wool rug. Weaver, Lila Winn.

Fig. 2-11. Detail of the double, plaited fringe on black, gray, and white rug. (Photographs of Figs. 2-10 and 2-11 by Kent Kammerer)

Another rug, woven by Mildred Sherwood, also has a design based on rectangles and squares, but with quite a different effect. It was woven entirely with Ghiordes knots tightly packed for a full, luxurious, evenly cut pile. The pattern of squares is put into a tawny background. Nearly all colors are used: reds, yellows, blues, and blue-greens. Figure C-4 in the color section shows a detail of this small jewel-like area rug.

Kathy Vinsonhaler wove a flat weave striped rug, but it is far from just another striped rug! (Figs. 2-12 and 2-13.) The contrast of black, cedar brown, and off-white handspun wools makes the most of the plain weave treadling sequence. Bands of striping with picket-fence edges combine with plain straight bands. In addition, the widest band, near the center, is of warm brown wool rounded and raised through the use of Oriental soumak rows packed in snugly. Some of the black stripes are woven in this technique, also. The linen warp ends are simply and neatly finished. A row of Philippine edge is worked across as a weft protector, then the warp ends are paired and twisted. A simple knot at the end holds the twist.

Fig. 2-12. Shadowed stripes on a wool rug. Weaver, Kathy Vinsonhaler.

Fig. 2-13. Close-up detail of the black, white, and brown rug showing the tightly packed soumak rows in a wide band. (Photographs of Figs. 2-12 and 2-13 by Beverly Rush)

While you are making a rug, you might just as well give yourself the bonus of two usable sides and a change in the color scheme. Two very different ways to weave a reversible rug follow.

With an 8-harness loom warped up in different colors, the number of possible intricate patterns and the reversals of color from one side to the other are more numerous than those on a 4-harness loom. The rug in Figure 2-14 was woven on an 8-harness Swiss loom and is about 60 in. wide. Handspun wool weft from Crete in natural grays is woven over a linen warp. The dramatic geometric pattern has the colors reversed on the opposite side.

Fig. 2-14. Reversible rug of handspun wool, woven on an 8-harness loom. Weaver, Sue Ann Kendall. (Photograph by Stuart Kendall)

TWO PILE WEAVE FACES

The four-harness 3/1 twill weave produces a fabric with two different faces. (Figs. 2-15 and 2-16.) Add some pile weave to both sides during the weaving, and you have quite a production. This is a small bedside rug in bright red, white, and two shades of blue. A lot of shaggy red and white pile on a bright blue ground is on one side; some light blue and a bit of red pile on the white and blue side. The warp is white, so the end fringes are white. The selvedges have random short weft fringe. Warp and weft are both acrylic rug yarn, so the rug is washable. This same weave and yarn size in wool, cotton, or acrylic can be worked out in any color plan you wish. Add pile or not. Because it is a weft-face weaving, your pattern is achieved by the play of weft colors and the treadling. The overshot is alternately over three warps, and then over one warp. Do a bit of sampling to find out just what happens to the weft colors on each side. Because the wefts pack in, this technique is a very good one for firm rugs and has the added attraction of a different look when the rug is reversed.

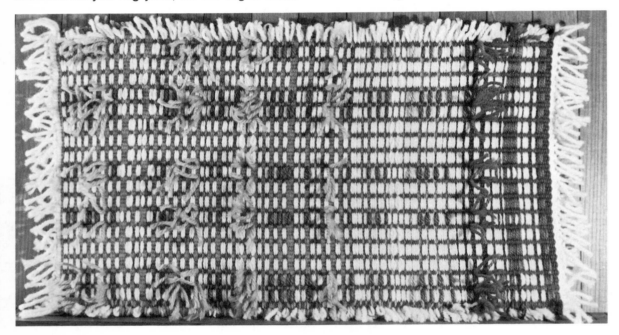

Fig. 2-15. Above: One side of the small reversible bedside rug with pile weave on both sides. This side is mostly blue and white.

Fig. 2-16. Below: The red and blue side of the bedside rug. Woven by author. (Photographs of Figs. 2-15 and 2-16 by Kent Kammerer)

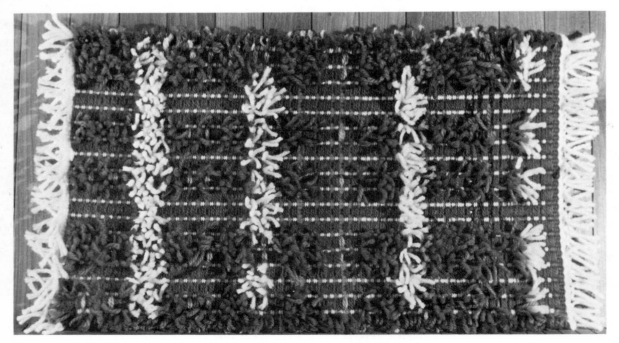

PUTTING IN THE TWO-FACED PILE

A two-faced pile can be accomplished, using the Icelandic cut pile, the Ghiordes knot, Sehna, Egyptian cut pile or laid in, simply by pushing the ends down through where your pattern requires, weaving tabby rows, then weaving the knots for the top surface. I have found it is easier to do on a frame loom, but it works on a floor loom, also. I have read directions elsewhere for putting in the second pile face on a textile after it is woven, but since the operation can be a part of the original weaving, I favor weaving both sides at once.

CARVED PILE

Call it carved, sculptured, contoured, or sheared —clipping a closely woven pile surface is exciting and puts your weaving into a deeper dimension. The beautifully sculptured Chinese rugs with patterns in low relief are fine models to examine. While our example is a study for a headboard, all the directions for weaving apply to rug making as well. A solid ground weave is necessary to support the heavy pile, so warps should be strong and close together.

The example in Figure 2-17 was woven in solidly packed Ghiordes knot. To make more wefts per inch, I used four or five strands as one, with a variation on the usual Ghiordes knot spacing. Borrow one warp from the previous pair as you make each successive knot, so each pair of warps contains one and one half knots, as seen in the drawing at right. Set your warp as close as you can without letting it become distorted by the weft. Know the maximum depth you will want for the highest point of carving, so there will be enough yarn length left for the lowest. Contouring does call for some practice, so you will have the right length of standing weft to cut and shape, as well as the right amount packed in per inch to give a tight, velvety surface.

Figure 2-17 shows part of a study for a woven headboard, and I tried different weights and spins of wool yarn as well as different weaves from flat plain weave through Oriental soumak for a slightly raised texture and Greek soumak for a higher woven surface. (See Fig. 6-22 for the rest of the weaving.) The full cut pile is sculptured, rounded, and clipped to different levels. Wool knitting worsted, when sheared, seems to give the smoothest result. The white areas on the right are of worsted. The white yarn in the left-side pattern is a tight, uneven handspun wool. The darker yarns are all very heavy, smooth handspun Greek yarns and Swedish plied rug yarn. Part of your experimentation with this technique should include using many kinds of yarn.

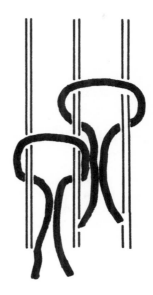

GHIORDES KNOT VARIATION

Fig. 2-17. A detail of carved pile weave, this example woven in Ghiordes knot is packed in tightly, with each warp pair holding one and one-half knots. Ground weaves are Greek soumak for medium-high textures, Oriental soumak, and plain weave. By author. (Photograph by Harold Tacker)

TIPS ON WEAVING
FOR SHEARING AND CARVING

It's not advisable to plunge right in with scissors on a finished piece. Better to do some small, less important ones first to learn the procedures.

Your snipping will give you quite a mass of wool that is even too short for a thrifty weaver to use as thrums. Save it to use as stuffing in pillows, pincushions, or any small padded areas.

You can tell if your yarn is too thick or your knots too large for the warp spaces when the warp is distorted or pushed out of line. For example: 16 warp ends per inch, woven in pairs, with a weft of doubled rug wool, in Greek soumak with three knots per warp, lapped over the next pair of warps. By knotting over every other warp pair, the weaving went into place without bulging or distortion.

By warping 8 e.p.i., doubled, you have the option of weaving on single warps (16 e.p.i.); 8 pairs per inch; or every other warp pair for 4 e.p.i.

In a crowded area, it is best to put several single weft knots over the same warp instead of several wefts in a single knot. It packs in better.

Remember that the cut ends of wool yarn look darker than loops or a flat weave, so consider this when selecting your colors.

Just as in tapestry weaving, you have to think ahead on color changes and design lines, shapes, and depths of the standing weft.

For even more packing-in of wefts, leave out an occasional tabby row and offset the next knot row. A no-tabby pile weave is too stretchy for a rug.

The surface of the area rug by Fritzi Oxley is luxuriously covered with cut and uncut pile surfaces and contoured forms of closely packed wool. (Fig. 2-18.) The shading and directional quality in the rocks, the flowing stream, and mossy banks is done with a sure touch. The contours gain their dimension from the shadows as well as actual relief carving. The rug was done in a combination of needle techniques related to weaving, including Ghiordes knot and hooking.

SHAPED RUGS

Shaped rugs are good design problems. Think of a rug as a space-filler on the floor either to cover an area completely or to define a traffic pattern or seating arrangement. Weave an accent rug with rounded corners, eccentric shaping, or an L-shape to fit a furniture grouping. A long hallway would be covered in a more imaginative way by a long rectangle with sections expanded out into each doorway. Let the shape on the floor come from units woven to be arranged and rearranged for a different shape and variation of pattern as suggested on page 27. Or put some woven shapes together like a jigsaw puzzle. A rug doesn't have to be just a single isolated square or rectangle.

Fig. 2-18. "Stream." Carved pile and looped and cut pile surfaces on an area rug by Fritzi Oxley. (Photograph by Beverly Rush)

Chapter 3

Walls, Windows, Screens, and Room Dividers

Each room has walls and windows usually in need of some fabric for privacy, acoustics, or enrichment. Spaces are just waiting for hand-wovens and creative solutions. A few are shown to start you off on ideas for your own use.

WALL COVERINGS

Woven wall coverings do not have to be limited to wall hangings or tapestries. Judy Thomas wove panels, which are installed as a complete wall covering, from floor to ceiling. (Fig. 3-1.) Each width of fabric is stretched in a light frame. Quite easily demountable, these panels have already been installed in two houses! Since they are mounted in separate frames, you can take them with you and can rearrange them if necessary in a new location. Double weave gives a firm solid fabric. The gray and black linen warp is woven with the same colors in a variety of patterns—stripes, broken stripes, rectangles, and squares of alternating unwoven and woven warp. These panels could also be used as a screen, since the double weave is equally attractive on the other side. A woven wall like this should give you lots of ideas. For example, it is a good way to change a wall surface or correct an awkward window or wall proportion.

Clara Chapman thought she wanted a grasscloth-covered wall in her new home —until she priced it! Her yarn supply yielded an assortment of beautiful linen and linen/silk in natural shades, so she designed and wove the rich, handsome wall covering in Swedish lace loom pattern shown in Figure 3-2. Her warp is three sizes of five different threads in light to dark natural beige colors. The weft is 8/1 natural linen, about the size of the heaviest warp thread.

Clara says, "My random ways in shade and texture helped to play down the seams, as did the horizontal pattern in the weft." She even covered the electrical outlet plate with fabric so it wouldn't glare! When the yardage was finished, she thoroughly soaked it in the bathtub, with five changes of water, then damp-dried and pressed it. The "paper hanger" had no trouble putting it up, and there was no shrinkage at the seams after application. This is a true weaver's approach to weaving you can use and enrichment of your home background!

Fig. 3-1. Movable panels in frames attached as a complete wall covering are shown in an overall view and a close-up detail. By weaver Judy Thomas. (Photograph by Harold Tacker)

Fig. 3-2. This linen and silk woven wall textile was installed like wallpaper. Woven by Clara Chapman. (Photograph by Harold Tacker)

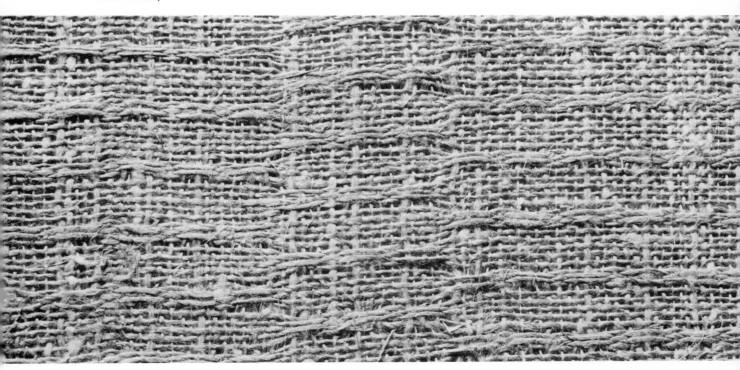

WALL HANGINGS

In this era when exhibits, books and other publications are over-endowed with wall hangings, I have chosen to include only a very few in this book. Wall hangings are such perfect mediums for experimenting with new techniques and playing with different effects and new materials. I think the following ones contribute something in the realm of design or use of material.

Bright, beautiful, and interesting to study time and again is the leather and yarn wall hanging by Lu Sever. (Fig. 3-3.) For some time Lu has been working with leather and woven wool in combination. She has used these two materials in bedspreads and other wall hangings as well as capes and umbrellas. This colorful piece, one of a "Flappy Bird" series, shows many yarn techniques combined with layers and shapes of leather. It somehow suggests one of Lu's capes, or perhaps it is related to some other rich vestment. A rod run through tabs along the top is a suitable and simple hanger. (See also Fig. C-7 in the color section.)

The completely understated hanging in Figure 3-4 is shown because of its beautiful simplicity. At the top, three embroidery hoops with heavily wrapped cords woven in are worked into the plain-weave background. The long ends—casually tied, but with a fine sense of composition—hang in graceful loops. They fall against the plain ground and end in long tassels. All white, the hanging is photographed against the light so that the pattern is darkly silhouetted.

I have just begun to explore the fascinating idea of big panels of much enlarged familiar loom patterns. Three from my first series, "Big Twills," are pictured in Figure 3-5. The three weavings are a standard diagonal twill and a diamond twill woven in brown and white wool. The third one was woven in blue and white wool because it is the three-harness jeans twill system used for weaving the familiar blue jeans fabric. A fourth one will be a more elaborate diamond or herringbone twill. In the photograph, the fourth space was filled with a few favorite weaving shuttles and yarn.

Each panel is 28 in. × 28 in. The twills were woven on squares of ½ in.-thick insulating board, as the loom, with big bundles of wool for warp and weft. As many as 20 strands are used as one. The white wool is from a "cheese" of very fine unspun wool rolag. The brown warps are a dozen strands of brown wool used as one. The warp ends are stapled to the top and bottom of the board, into the thickness of it. This same idea of expanded loom patterns could be more easily worked out on a large floor loom, but I thought this experiment was worth the effort.

Fig. 3-3. "Flappy Bird" wall hanging in leather and woven wool. Also see Figure C-7 for the warm, rich colors. Weaver, Luana Sever. (Photograph by Beverly Rush)

Fig. 3-4. White wall hanging silhouetted against the sky. Woven by Judy Thomas. (Photograph by Paul Thomas)

This is fun! I can see a whole wall of these panels, and believe they would be a very good teaching help because the path of the pattern yarn is easily traced.

You can fill a wall with large panels of "Grafics," as Gloria Crouse did. (See Fig. C-9 in the color section.) Almost op art, and related to big painted graphics in color and composition, these four works have the added dimension of texture in the weaves, plus circles, squares, stripes, and balanced colors. Bold geometric shapes are woven in tapestry techniques within the square shape of each piece. Because they are mounted on stiff backing with no frame, all of the attention is on the woven designs. They could be arranged on a wall in any number of ways.

Fig. 3-5. "Big Twills." These expanded twills include the diagonal, diamond, and the three-harness blue-jeans twill. By author. (Photograph by Beverly Rush)

The two small wall hangings in Figures 3-6 and 3-9 are studies in padded double weave and show some of the potential of this technique. Seat pads, cushions, comforters are a few other uses of this method which does so much for you. The reverse side of double-weave items is often as attractive but different from the other surface, so it is an excellent choice for weaving space dividers or anything that will be seen from both sides. Also, double weave can be enjoyed with one side out, then the other, for a change of scene. Both sides of the Chilkat-source hanging were photographed to show what happened on each side. (Figs. 3-6 through 3-8.) Nanci Hansen went to the traditional Chilkat blanket for her design source. The hanging's long fringe tapers to a point, and the patterned areas suggest the Chilkat twined patterns. A further tie to Northwest Indian design is the cedar bark color of the wool and long fringe which has the look of fringed cedar bark skirts and rain capes. Natural gray and white handspun wools and some red-purple are added in the small patterns. The brown warp layer is the long, full fringe; the gray warp layer is woven in long tabs.

Fig. 3-6. Front of the double-weave padded hanging. Source of design was a Chilkat blanket.

Fig. 3-7. Back view of the cedar brown and natural gray wool hanging.

Fig. 3-8. Detail of the front center section of the padded hanging. By weaver Nanci Hansen. (Photographs of Figs. 3-6, 3-7, and 3-8 by Beverly Rush)

Lew Gilchrist wove "Blue Window" in deep blue with some green and natural gray wool and a bit of brilliant scarlet for accent. (Figs. 3-9 and 3-10.) The double weave was stuffed as it was woven, then finished with wrapped warp end fringe and tassels. The "window" is formed by wrapped warps over a plain weave layer at the back. Stuffed tubular weave forms the padded columns, with slits between which separate the padded columns for a slightly architectural look.

Another stuffed and quilted wall decoration is the sunny yellow tactile hanging by Jill Nordfors in Figure 3-11. Although this sunshine-yellow padded hanging is not woven, it does include a great deal of Ghiordes knot pile, and the fat French knots might be woven loops. It is such good design and contains so many ideas for changes in textures that it will be an inspiration to weavers. Well known for her exquisite stitcheries and appliqués, Jill Nordfors also has stimulating ideas for weavers. She made this hanging for a tactile exhibit. She used knitted fabric for the ground, stuffed it with dacron, and quilted it for plump areas. Besides the cut pile, she included French knots, applique of smooth satin, and several detached stitches.

Fig. 3-9. "Blue Window" is a stuffed double-weave hanging with shaped fringe and tassels.

Fig. 3-10. Detail of the "window" showing the wrapped warps. Weaver, Lew Gilchrist. (Photographs of Figs. 3-9 and 3-10 by Beverly Rush)

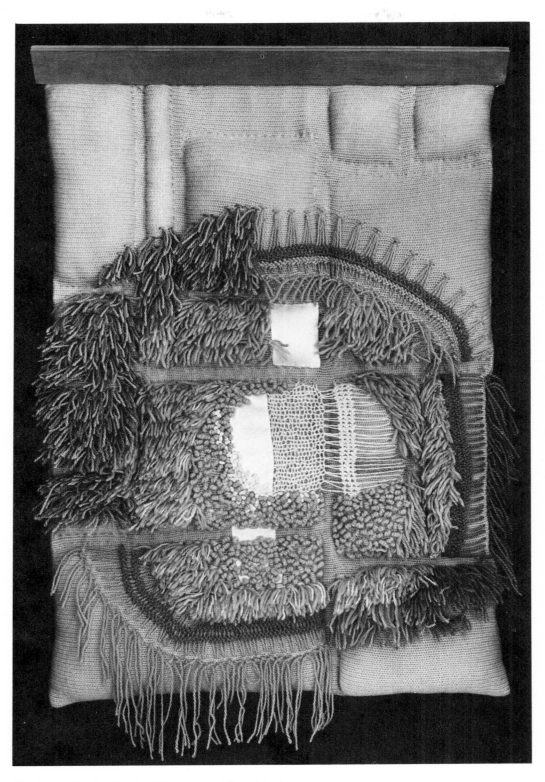

Fig. 3-11. "Tactile Hanging" has many different texture
levels, from slick satin to deep cut pile. By Jill Nordfors.
(Photograph by Beverly Rush)

TAPESTRIES

Whether large and loosely hung or framed, or small and mounted or simply hung on the wall, tapestries have a time-honored place and use. I differentiate between tapestries and wall hangings because to me a tapestry is woven in the traditional plain weave tapestry, with all of the nuances of color change and blending, or in the single soumak or other soumak techniques. However, while the techniques are traditional, modern tapestries do not necessarily have to follow the tradition of exacting pictorial representation. On the contrary, the use of our heritage of tapestry methods makes possible the expression of abstract and nonrepresentational work and can be expanded by use of other techniques for a desired texture. Just two small tapestries are included here to suggest that these, too, have a definite use on walls. They are perfect little jewel-like accents, or may be effective in a whole wall of weavings, prints, paintings, and objects. I have consistently urged weavers to try their skills on small tapestries *at first*, so that they will not be dismayed at the length of time required for this painstaking technique when they are confronted with a large design.

My interest in the Coptic portraits woven so long ago in Egypt resulted in the "Coptic Saint" in Figure 3-12. (See also Fig. C-3 in the color section.) Although he is woven in plain tapestry, with some soumak for texture and with a Greek soumak border, the pictorial style, with large eyes and simplified details, is similar to that of the Copts.

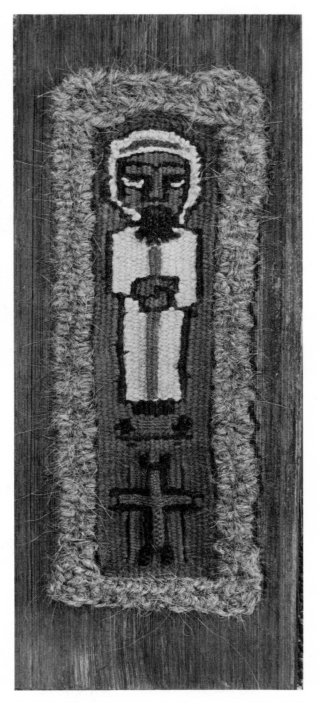

Fig. 3-12. "Coptic Saint" is a fugitive from the Ethnic Wall Rug (see Fig. 2-3). We put him on a thick, weathered hand-split cedar board and left him out of the composition. By author. (Photograph by Kent Kammerer)

The faces in Figure 3-13 were woven in a combination of techniques—mainly plain weave tapestry and single soumak. (See Fig. C-5 in the color section.) Other methods were used where needed for a special effect. This small tapestry was great fun, since I never knew who was coming up next. After choosing yarn for the hair and skin color, each person just seemed to emerge in the allotted space! Try a project like this—I think you will enjoy it! The Coptic Saint was mounted on weathered, hand-split cedar, about an inch thick. "The Girls," with its narrow woven border, is backed with felt and hung with no visible rod.

Fig. 3-13. "The Girls." Faces woven in several tapestry and pile weave techniques, with a woven border. By author. (Photograph by Kent Kammerer)

HOW TO WEAVE A BORDER ON A TAPESTRY

Weaving a border around a tapestry gives a finished, complete look. The weaving looks framed, but the edging is harmonious because it is of yarn. Gothic tapestries, woven in such quantity during the twelfth to sixteenth centuries, often were bordered. Some were simple narrow edges of plain weave in a dark color. As the tapestries became more and more elaborate, the borders also became ornate, woven to give the illusion of a carved wooden frame or with faces, cherubs, flowers, scrolls, columns, or arches surrounding the detailed scene in the center. Deep borders sometimes had the story of the tapestry painstakingly woven in, so the complete tale depicted was explained. A modern miniaturized tapestry will also benefit from a border kept to the small scale of the pattern.

Consider the woven margin as part of your total design. Some weavings seem to need the definite line around the edge, and others are best without. Adding a border as you weave is not difficult, but it is more time consuming than a plain selvedge. It requires two color changes in each row of weaving and consistent joining at the color change points at each side border. Long slits should be avoided as the weight of the hanging will cause them to open and sag. The directions that follow are general and apply to any weaving that has a woven edge as trim or frame—and to any technique used, whether plain weave or one of the surface texture weaves. I often use Greek soumak for a border because of the raised texture which sets off a plain weave tapestry and gives some depth. Other ways to vary a woven frame is to use doubled or larger yarn in either plain weave or a knot technique.

TO WEAVE

Begin the weaving with rows all the way across in the border color and technique, weaving up the depth of the bottom border. You will need two separate border wefts in bobbins or small shuttles to weave up each side. The right and left sides will be woven at the same time as the central section. Keep the border rows even with the center. For example: From the left, weave over the number of warps for the edge; interlock the border weft with the center weft; weave the center section row; interlock with the weft of the right-hand border and weave that edge. To return from right to left, weave the right border width; the center and the left border. Continue in this fashion until the weaving is complete and ready for the top border, which is woven as the bottom border was, all the way across up to the depth required for the top edge.

The joining techniques are any of those used in plain weave tapestry at the color-change point. Use the one that fits into your overall scheme for the effect you want: interlocked for an inconspicuous smooth join; single dovetail for a fine and subtle toothed join, or multiple dovetail for a serrated joining pattern. Double interlock results in a ridged joining, especially when it is done on the surface rather than the classic method woven from the reverse side. A minimal slit of only two or three rows will give a dotted-line effect and when slits are so small, will not pull and distort the weaving. When the yarn is thin and the joins are single and pulled flat, the border will blend into the center weaving. When an offset border is desired, any technique that will raise the yarn, create ridges, or a thick surface should be chosen. Still another way to contrast the border and central pattern is by a strong color contrast. Use any of these methods for whatever effect you strive for to border your tapestry, whether it is an abstract pattern or representational. If your frame is woven in one of the knotted techniques, the center section weft is the joining weft and will be taken around one or two warps above and below each knot. The actual joining will be concealed by the knots. Three shuttles or bobbins are employed just for the two borders and the center weaving. Additional color changes in the middle section will require more, so weaving a border does take more time and uses more motions of putting down and taking up additional colors.

Look at museum tapestries and photographs of the heroic weavings from the past for ideas on borders. A woven frame around a fine tapestry is well worth the extra planning, design, and weaving time.

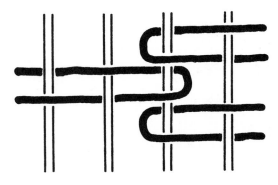

SINGLE DOVETAIL JOINING

A strong abstract pattern in simple black and white wool was woven in the classic plain-weave tapestry technique, with dovetail joinings. (Fig. 3-14.) The design is by Evelyn Ackerman and the weaving was done in Mexico. The bottom edge is finished in typical fashion, with warp ends knotted and clipped very close. The top edge is stapled to a strip of dark-stained wood. This work is a good example of simplicity, both in the weaving and the limited color without any color blending.

Hella Skowronski's large tree tapestry, which covers a wall, is handsome and richly colored in browns and autumn colors against cream-white. (Fig. 3-15.) Although the work was commissioned for a large office building, it would also be a great addition to a home. It is presented as an idea for filling a whole wall, perhaps above a long buffet or chest. The technique used is mostly Greek soumak, with variations.

Fig. 3-14. Black and white wool plain-weave tapestry. Courtesy Mr. and Mrs. Gary Wilson. (Photograph by Harold Tacker)

Fig. 3-15. A tapestry big enough to fill a wall shows a stately stand of trees, woven in Greek soumak with variations. By Hella Skowronski.

Fig. 3-16. Hooking, needlework, and appliqué blended into a charming tapestrylike view of Paris. By Helen J. Rumpel. (Photograph by Beverly Rush)

The pictorial wall hanging in Figure 3-16 is composed of many techniques: hooking, appliqué, and stitchery, with loops, couching, and beads for raised textures. This playful view of Paris could have been woven in plain and pile weaves. It is presented for your enjoyment and for the folk-art style and subject.

A WEAVER'S EXERCISE
IN 16-HARNESS POINT TWILL

Ruth Rummler wove 153 treadlings in 16-harness point twill as samplers, then hung them as a wall decoration. (Fig. 3-17.) Beautifully woven in a pleasant green, with the patterns in white, this is a wall hanging with continuing interest. I couldn't resist using the samplers as a table textile suggestion in Figure 7-11—they fit in so perfectly with that favorite use of sampler strips. Using such strips as decoration and reference will enrich your surroundings, too.

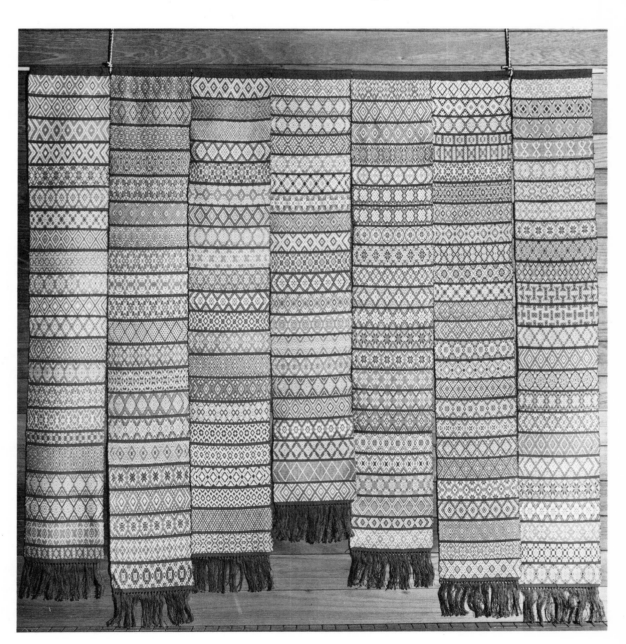

Fig. 3-17. 153 different treadlings in 16-harness point twills by expert weaver Ruth Rummler. (Photograph by Harold Tacker)

WINDOW COVERINGS

Not much on conventional casement cloth, draperies, and curtains has been included in this text only because of limited space and the desire to show some less usual weavings, but these fabrics probably play an even larger part than wall coverings in the whole scheme of weaving you can use in your home. They can be woven in any weight you require, from very open, lacy weaves to the heaviest which solidly cover the space. Colors and textures can be chosen to exactly fit your needs. Figures 3-18 and 3-19 provide two examples of beautifully woven casement cloth by Hella Skowronski. Her designing of curtain fabrics for commercial producers has helped to make good designs available to nonweavers. The sheer casement cloth in Figure 3-19 was used in a surprising way—in a provocative gown for Cleopatra's attendant in the movie of the same name.

Other ways to cover or decorate your walls and windows with plain or patterned fabric follow. These ways of using lengths of fabric also serve to unify a room with oddly proportioned windows, or with other architectural details that are best covered.

Weave related panels in whatever size fits the space best. Hang them loose from rods like a drapery or stretch them in light frames. Hang them side by side or at intervals.

Hang the panels in sections and surround them with a frame of simple molding fastened to the wall. Borrow from and update the brocade walls seen in the decades of elaborate wall decor.

Return to the original use of huge tapestries and hang pictorial or patterned weavings in deep folds from large hooks on the wall.

Stretch your fabric into light frames and hang them from a curtain track so that they can slide over a window or over a wall, as needed, like the Japanese fusuma and shogi.

Another way is to hang a flat width on a decorative rod: Put pairs of brackets on the wall and at the window. When window shading is desired, place the rod on the window brackets. When shading is not needed, remove the rod to matching brackets on a wall and have a wall hanging. This idea can be expanded for use with several layers of panels. Weaving some layers see-through and some solid builds a wall hanging with depth, which, however, also separates to cover several windows with single panels.

Another way to cover windows, walls, or archways, improve the acoustics, and soften a large space is this: Weave sections of drapery in heavy, light, and sheer weights on the same warp. Hang them so heavier panels cover windows and lighter-weight sections cover the

wall, for a continuous covering. A sheer section can be placed over a window where the privacy of a dense weave is not needed. Great color-play is possible, as well as pattern build-up.

To create an illusion of more windows and use maximum light from existing narrow windows, hang panels of fabric at the edge of the window frame, covering the wall to a corner or between windows. The panels can be in frames, as noted, or hung loose from a rod.

Just one panel can be patterned or pictorial, in pick-up, laid-in, a loom-pattern, or tapestry weave, with the larger areas covered with plain or textured cloth in blending colors and duplicate yarns. (Fig. 3-20.)

For window screening that will let in some light but give privacy, too, use woven bands together with hairpin lace or joined with an airy, lacy stitch. Horizontal or vertical bands can be hung on a rod. Vertical bands can be suspended from a curtain track and pushed back and forth.

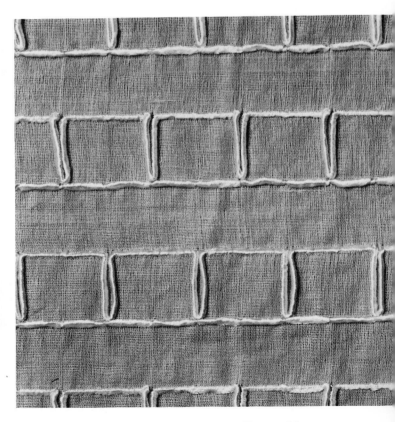

Fig. 3-18. The natural and white casement, "Terrace," is made of linen/mohair and satiny acetate chenille. Woven by Hella Skowronski.

SLAT BLINDS

Slats of plastic, bamboo, or wood, woven with spaced warp in stripes of wool, jute, chenille, or linen, give filtered or very little light, depending upon the frequency of warp spacing. Hella Skowronski developed slat blinds from a special, rigid fiberglass material and used chenilles, silks, and other exotic yarns for warp, including leather, chains, and beads. The roll-up blind in Figure 3-21, with its warps of leather strips and wool, was made to fit into the window frame. The roll is toward the window, and a separately woven valance covers the top edge so the installation is very smooth and tailored.

Fig. 3-19. The sheer glass curtain, with horizontal bands of heavier weave, hangs in full folds from floor to ceiling. By Hella Skowronski. (Photograph by Art Hupy)

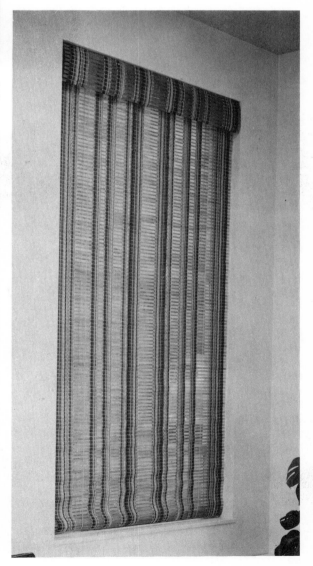

Fig. 3-20. Handwoven linen draperies flank a panel of sheer linen with a laid-in pattern silhouetted against the light. By Harold and Sylvia Tacker. (Photograph by Harold Tacker)

Fig. 3-21. Slat blinds with leather and wool. Weaver, Hella Skowronski. (Photograph by Alexandre Georges)

WARP/SCREEN

Morning summer sun caused some heat and glare on my desk for a few hours, so some screening was called for. Not wanting a permanently installed curtain or shade, I made a warp/screen. (Figs. 3-22 and 3-23.) When the sun moves on, the screen is lifted off the window and put on two wall hooks. The wall is enhanced and my view of trees and water is opened. At the same moment, we are speaking the weaver's language of love of yarn—and about a non-weaving!

Do you sometimes make up a warp that is so pretty by itself that you don't want to cover it with weft? This idea stemmed from that one, along with the need for a screen made quickly on-the-spot. Here is a scheme for an almost instant screen.

The basics of the warp/screen idea are these:

To provide a screen by fastening warps on a hanger.

To devise a movable screen, easily put up or taken away, and perhaps temporary, therefore—

Fast to assemble. After these points are fulfilled, you can tailor the project to your situation. Within the bounds of the simple plan, you will find an extraordinary number of applications and variations.

Another good reason to make a screen like this is for help in designing drapery fabric. Hang the warp in the window, study it, live with it awhile, and you might visualize the fabric. You still can change yarns, colors, warp sequence—and your mind!

Collect some of the most interesting yarns you can find to fasten to the rod for the screen. It can be sized to fit a doorway, a window, or hung free from the ceiling or out from wall or window. Fill the space from rod to windowsill, or to the floor.

The holder can be almost anything appropriate to the installation: a length of carved molding from the hardware store; a strip of wood or dowel; a brass bar, rod, or curtain rod. If the warp/screen is a permanent part of your window and will be out of the way part of the time, just slip the warps through the holes in the drapery slides on a traverse rod and knot them. It will pull back just like a drapery does.

The yarns can be a mixture of almost anything that appeals to you. They should hang well. The softer ones hang more gracefully than the wiry fibers. Select different weights, textures, spins, fibers, and colors. Choose for harmony and to suit your particular need. Use some of the same yarns you put into your rugs, upholstery, or other drapery.

More advantages:

A soft screening such as this will take away a bald, unfinished look of a window that does not require a full drapery treatment. A small amount of precious fiber can be displayed this way until you decide how you want to use it in a weaving.

The project is twofold and the advantages are many: It is speedy, expedient, a showcase for lovely yarns, serves a purpose, and is quite expendable and recyclable. So compose a gorgeous warp, hang it up, and enjoy it!

Fig. 3-22. Warp/screen to filter strong light. By author.

VARIATIONS ON THE THEME

Unwoven warp on a rod is just like a warp-weighted loom where the warp is hung from a top beam. As an extension of the simple rod and warp idea, weights can be hung along the bottom of the strands. Thread on weighty beads, fish weights, wooden shapes, or something small but heavy enough to put a small amount of tension on the strands. The weights will help if you wish to twine a few rows or weave an inch or so at the top. Moving still further from simplicity, some of the strands can be knotted or braided, but then you approach a different treatment and are creating a woven hanging.

All chenille yarns in two or three sizes will make a dense warp/screen with a luxurious velvety texture when closely spaced.

A light, delicate effect is created by very fine white silk or wool spaced about ¼ in. apart. A tiny unobtrusive lead weight will keep each strand hanging straight. The look is of rain running down the glass.

The step beyond the weighted warp is to stretch the warps in a light frame, but leave them unwoven. Then you have a warp all ready to weave if you care to, later on.

HOW TO ASSEMBLE A WARP/SCREEN

These directions explain how I did the warp/screen for my study window, but you can adapt them to your own project by your choice of holder, yarns, method, and place of hanging, and measurements to fit your space.

Measure from rod to windowsill. Wrap one strand around the rod to measure how much is needed for the hitch, then measure off lengths of warp twice the length from rod to sill plus the wrapping. Put each single strand around the holder in a lark's head hitch. As the drawing shows, double the length of warp, evening up the ends, and put the loop under the bar with loop toward you. Bring the two cut ends down through the loop and pull to tighten. For a better hang and a line of yarn for a heading, have the loop cross over on the front side.

LARK'S HEAD HITCH

Fig. 3-23. Detail of the carved molding and the warp looped around it. (Photographs of Figs. 3-22 and 3-23 by Harold Tacker)

The holder chosen was a length of carved molding about an inch wide. The grooves in the pattern automatically space the warps. (See Fig. 3-23.) The yarns are in three shades of blue-green, yellow, yellow-green, cream, and beige the color of the light wood. A few strands of red-orange echo the orange chair and shelf brackets, and deep blue strands, the rug color. The yarns, from fine bouclé through rug wool, braided wool, thick and thin handspun, and plied wools, create a line silhouette of fibers, while sifting the light. The strands were placed in a casually planned order. One more advantage to this method—your strands can easily be rearranged if your first try is not pleasing. No end weights were required here, and the warp/screen hangs well. If any yarns are inclined to twist and crimp too much, a few passes with a steam iron will straighten them out.

Because the screen is very lightweight, only two 1½-inch wire brads hold it in place. Holes were drilled through the molding, into the window mullion. The brads extend about an inch, are inconspicuous, and the screen very easily slips on and off from them.

SCREENS AND ROOM DIVIDERS

The use of handwovens to divide space in a room, suggest a visual division, screen off an undesirable view, or veil a window for privacy offers a perfect design problem for a weaver. You can do just about anything you wish with color, pattern, texture, and size. The screens and dividers discussed do these chores in a variety of ways and will serve to start you off. Almost every home has at least one place in need of this kind of treatment!

Sue Ann Kendall's dramatic room divider, "Le Monde en Ronde," is deceptively simple in design. (Fig. 3-24.) The divider is nearly 6 ft. wide and 10 ft. tall, but the idea could be scaled down to fit into a smaller space. All handspun wool, with warp and weft in natural grays, the piece was woven on the same loom as the rug in Figure 2-14. The 8-harness weave reverses the pattern colors on the other side. Heavy metal bars at top and bottom help to keep the divider hanging true and steady. This is a shaped weaving in reverse, since the unwoven warps become the main pattern with a woven shape surrounding them.

A divider from counter height to ceiling gives just a suggestion of screening. (Fig. 3-25.) All in brown and amber tones, the wide-apart straps of woven jute are held together by a few rows of unusual weft materials: strips of smooth cedar bark, copper tubes, and amber beads in two sizes. These materials are almost trademarks of Hella Skowronski's innovative woven blinds and dividers.

Karen Vanderpool wove an effective window screen or room divider, using leno technique with macramé finish at each end. (Figs. 3-26 and 3-27.) Natural linen is the foil for black jute, which outlines a flowing pattern and is used for some of the weft. Openings in the weave create more interest, especially when the weaving is hung in a window. The mounting and end finish are particularly well thought out and accomplished. Black warp ends are worked into a short length of macramé over the natural colored ends, surrounding them, and give the effect of beads in the center. The light ends hang in a straight fringe. At the top, the light linen warp ends are cut to stand in a perky row. Top and bottom edges are inserted between two half-rounds that were painted flat black.

The kind of screening represented by this piece is very versatile; it can be hung in a glass doorway, in a window, or can be used to section off part of a room.

Fig. 3-24. "Le Monde en Ronde" by weaver Sue Ann Kendall is a grand peek-through space divider, woven on an 8-harness loom. (Photograph by Harold Tacker)

Fig. 3-25. "Amber" is an open screen of bands with just enough wefts to hold them together and add sparkle with the clear amber beads. By weaver Hella Skowronski. (Photograph by Art Hupy)

Fig. 3-26. Precise pattern in a linen and jute window screen or room divider.

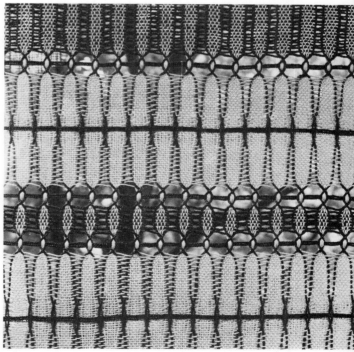

Fig. 3-27. Detail of the linen and jute leno-weave screen, with macramé-end finish. Woven by Karen Vanderpool. (Photographs of Figs. 3-26 and 3-27 by Beverly Rush)

61

Reminiscent of romantic bead curtains, the door hanging in Figures 3-28 and 3-29 reflects a much more sophisticated approach to a flexible, walk-through door covering. (See also Fig. C-13 in the color section.) A few inches of double weave at the top provides a tube for inserting the brass rod hanger. Then the double weave is separated and woven into strips which ebb and flow, twist, and join in a completely fascinating pattern of line and color. Just two colors are used—a rich red-purple and deep-gold rug wool. At different lengths the weaving stops and warps are wrapped. Occasionally a chunky hand-formed bead is slipped onto the warp. The ends are all wrapped in a deep oval loop. This wrapped-loop end finish dates back to the Bronze Age. After wrapping the warp strands down as far as you care to, divide the warps into two groups and tie the ends together. Continue the wrapping down one side of the loop, covering the knot, and up, where the end of the wrapping yarn can be run into the wrapping and clipped.

This weaving by Verla Christianson is also versatile because it would be equally effective against a window or hanging free anywhere in a room. Motion adds even more interest to this imaginative panel. I saw the work in progress on the loom and it was definitely not a happening; it was very carefully planned.

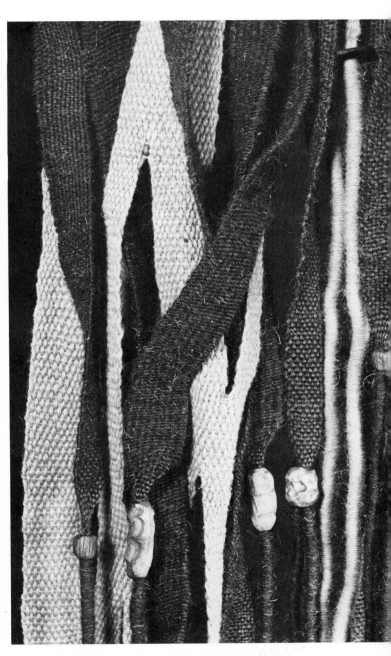

Fig. 3-28. A walk-through door hanging weaves and twists down to the wrapped warp ends.

Fig. 3-29. A detail of the door hanging shows the intricate slit weave. By Verla Christianson. (Photographs of Figs. 3-28 and 3-29 by Beverly Rush)

Fig. 3-30. The South Coast Weavers' Guild screen has panels of individually woven textiles in stained-glass colors. (Photograph by Curtis and Betty Bell)

Fig. 3-31. A detail of the fabric in one section of the screen. Woven by members of the South Coast Weavers' Guild in Santa Ana, California. (Photograph by Karen Gartner)

MOVABLE SCREENS

Free-standing movable panel screens are another way to achieve temporary or permanent screening—across a corner, to separate a section of a room, or in a doorway. You design and weave a portable spot of textile richness, using a correlated pattern of tapestry panels or a variety of textures, patterns, and color. The screen can be opaque or solid, or have some transparency.

The South Coast Weavers' Guild in Southern California constructed the stunning four-part screen in Figures 3-30 and 3-31 for their exhibit at the Southern California Conference of Handweavers. (See also Fig. C-10 in the color section.) It was a rewarding exercise in total-member cooperation. Those who were not yet ready to weave for an exhibition felt encouraged to weave a small portion as part of the screen. The design, weaving, colors, and construction are expertly done. Although the screen was made for an exhibit and the black cut-out frame is of poster board, the same idea can very well be used with the frame cut out of wood. It is a sandwich construction, with the fabric put between the black poster board frame on the front and white poster board on the back layer. The panels are then fastened to a wooden four-panel, black-painted hinged frame. The frame has three horizontal bars across each panel which give strength and add something to the cutout pattern. Done to suggest stained glass, the weaving's semi-sheer areas show the various woven patterns and laid-in areas as the light streams through. An effective part of the whole design is the way the cutout frame extends up above the square basic screen. Rounded and filled with cloth, the extension adds a nice finishing touch and proportion.

This project is brimming with ideas and is a perfect group-participation undertaking for weavers with more or less experience.

FRAMED SCREENS

Two quite different screens, each in a frame: "Crystallyne"—soft, heavy, white rayon weft loops down between woven bands of close-set warp, with beads. (Fig. 3-32.) Each panel is hung in a shaped frame. The screen was arranged in a setting for a designer show, but the idea could be adapted for home use, either for a movable or stationary screen.

Figure 3-33 shows a screen with rigid fiberglass slats and brass rods of various sizes woven close together over narrow groups of warp, with an occasional open space between strips. The material is fastened into frames for a rigid, sturdy wall screen. Both framed screens were designed and woven by Hella Skowronski.

WINDOW HANGING

Barbara Chapman's semi-sheer window panel, "Trinity," was woven with natural linen warp and white wool weft and demonstrates an expert, full use of both the loom and weaver-controlled techniques. (Fig. 3-34.) Hung before an 8-ft. window, it forms a backdrop for a grand piano, with the surprise benefit of being an effective sound screen. It also softens the view of a boat-yard parking lot while filtering light into the high-ceilinged room. The overlay yarn for the trinity is handspun wool, heavier than the ground weave, which was redented and rethreaded to achieve the crossings. Danish medallion technique is the subtle pattern in the columns. The bottom hem is weighted with fish-line lead weights.

Fig. 3-32. "Crystallyne." Fabric was hung in a shaped screen of wood. Woven by Hella Skowronski. (Photograph by Vern and Elizabeth Green)

Fig. 3-33. A rigid woven screen in a frame has brass rods and fiberglass slats. Weaver, Hella Skowronski. (Photograph by Roger Dudley)

Fig. 3-34. "Trinity" is a linen and wool window-hanging which was woven to screen and filter the light from an 8-ft window. Weaver, Barbara Chapmen. (Photograph by Harold Tacker)

SPACE HANGINGS

A good model of effective screening without density was created for some spacious rooms in an older home that had been made into apartments. (See Fig. C-12 in the color section.) What had probably once been the large family dining room, with paneling and plate rail, had an alcove with a Murphy bed shut off from the room by French doors. The bed was taken out and a narrow kitchen installed. The doors were removed, leaving a wide archway looking into the kitchen and at the refrigerator. Sandra Hastings, an accomplished weaver, made a space hanging which she intended to stop the eye rather than fill all of the wide space. It allows passage on either side, but you are not too aware of the kitchen in the background because the weaving is so enchanting. She was inspired by mosses and trees, the landscape, and colors found in nature. Knotting and weaving techniques create a sculptured look, all in greens—from very dark to light yellow-green. The long, widely spaced, and grouped warp ends nearly reaching the floor and the irregular outline expand the airy quality of the loopy texture. This weaving does the work of arresting your glance short of the kitchen in a much more imaginative way than the more usual curtain, door, or flat panels.

The hanging in Figure 3-35 of Persian rug wool warp-face bands and narrow strips is useful as a space-filler on walls, hung free from the ceiling, or placed in a window. Because of the play of light and fabric, it is particularly interesting against a window or where it can be seen from all sides, lending a shadow when in a strong light. The colors are deep, quiet blues and purples with a bit of green. The technique is a version of demadesh, or slit weave, where groups of warps are woven with openings between. The woven areas join and separate and join again at a different place. The hanging resembles the double weave door hanging in Figure 3-28 but is a single-warp weave and is the same on both sides.

The two bands at the sides were woven separately. The middle section was woven on a wide band loom fitted with three small rigid heddles, side by side. The separated strips were woven simultaneously across the warp width, row by row, with the rigid heddles lifted in different combinations—three, two, or one at a time—to create the slits. The three separate lengths were assembled by joining in just a few places, leaving additional long slits between joins. The firm warp-faced band weave gives enough rigidity to the strips so they hang well.

Fig. 3-35. Slit-weave hanging of warp-face band weaving. By Sylvia and Harold Tacker. (Photograph by Harold Tacker)

Chapter 4

Furniture, Hammocks, and Swings

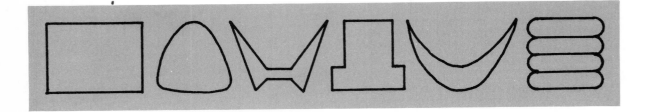

Usually, upholstery fabric is woven by the yard, carefully planned to have enough stretch—but not too much; a firm weave for long wear; and a weight that will tailor well and look right at seams and edges. Chairs or benches of an unusual shape, cushions with boxed edges, period-style chairs with inset panels of fabric—all these benefit from weaving-to-shape. The idea is far from new: Needlepoint upholstery is made to size and tapestries were made to fit chairs, sofas, and fire screens.

SHAPED WEAVING FOR FURNITURE

Once you have done some weaving to size and shape, you will have learned the procedures. Each problem will be slightly different, and only one will be detailed here. The methods used are the same no matter what size or shape you are weaving.

Loom-shaping upholstery or a pad for a chair is essentially the same process as that for weaving loom-shaped clothing. You measure carefully, make a pattern, then weave your cloth to fit the pattern.

Shaping an armhole or a neckline is an identical procedure. Employ the tapestry techniques of weaving on a slant, following the curves and sloping lines of the pattern. When straight lines are called for—for instance, when leaving out a square at a corner—weave back and forth, turning the weft around the warp that defines the edge. Continue weaving this edge until the shape requires widening again. The unwoven warp ends are disposed of in any of several ways, dictated by your specific weaving. They may be simply darned in, leaving a selvedge; worked into an edge finish; utilized for sewing parts together (see the pad in Figs. 4-3 and 4-4); lacing, tying, ends can be left as a fringe if this is appropriate—or whatever your creative hands choose to do with them and is suitable to your project. For example, when you weave a boxed cushion cover or chair seat with the corners unwoven, those unused warps will be used in the joining. Put the edges together, sew, lace, or tie the warps—put them together much as you made paper May baskets in elementary-school days! This method works well for a heavy upholstery fabric, since it eliminates cut edges and bulk at the corners, which you want straight and firm.

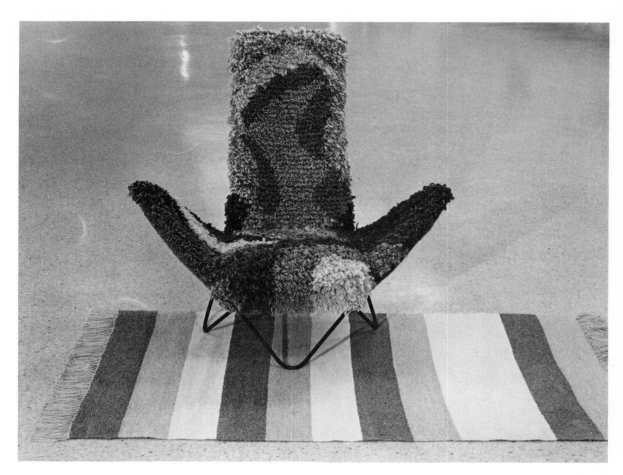

Fig. 4-1. "Chairwoman," a magnificent shaped weaving is all rya knots, in loops. The handspun wool is in natural colors, but some wool was dyed with birch and turmeric for soft green and yellow.

An expert level of shaped weaving and fabricating was attained by Kerstin Schweizer in her "Chairwoman" and rug, which express a thoroughly coordinated design. (Figs. 4-1 and 4-2.) The butterfly chair frame was modified by her husband; then she wove a richly luxurious padded cover for it. The yarns are handspun wool in natural grays and white, with a muted green and yellow from birch and turmeric dyes. All top surfaces are woven in Rya knot loops. The fabric on the entire back is flat weave in the natural gray wool.

The side pieces were shaped as woven on the loom. The seat and back sections were woven to size and shape. A soft padded cushion was made for the seat. To complete the picture, Kerstin Schweizer used the gray yarns to weave a rug with wide stripes which follow through visually up to the pattern in the chair.

Fig. 4-2. In the detail of the woven chair, note that the stripes in the flat-weave rug follow through up in the chair design. By weaver-spinner-dyer Kerstin Schweizer. (Photographs by Harold Tacker)

SHAPED CHAIR PAD

A shaped pad for an unyielding but very comfortable plastic circle chair was woven, both sides at once, on the same frame loom with just one warping. (Figs. 4-3 through 4-7.) The following directions can be adapted and used in a general way to weave a similar pad, a cushion, or shaped covering of any size or shape. Use a frame loom a few inches larger than your fabric will be and weave either a single layer or the two sides at once, as I did. The directions for planning, shaping, and weaving apply whether you are using a floor or a frame loom.

Fig. 4-3. Reversible shaped pad, woven to shape for the circle chair.

TO WEAVE A TWO-FACED PAD

First measure the chair seat and determine the size and shape of the area to be covered. Be sure your measurement allows enough for the finished pad to cover the chair edge adequately. Cut a paper pattern; heavy wrapping paper is a good choice for the pattern. Place the pattern between the warp layers where the outline will be followed as you weave. Think about what kind of an edge you want. I planned to slip the top and bottom members of the frame out, leaving loop warp ends as a fringe below the heading. This is an advantage of using a stretcher frame, since the corners simply come apart and you can choose between having the loop warp ends or cutting them.

Certain cautions and hints should be kept in mind as you weave:

Keep your wefts relaxed so the warp is not pulled in or distorted on either edge or on either warp. This care will give you a spongy but firmly woven fabric, in the true shape of your pattern, and make blocking unnecessary.

When wool warp matches the weft, the loop warp ends are a proper finish and do not need to be hidden or embellished. For a pad or cushion where fringe is unsuitable, the warp ends can be darned in.

If necessary, ties can be woven in to fasten the pad to the chair. The slope of the chair seat and the heaviness of this pad made tying unnecessary; the pad stays in place very well.

Variations: One side could have been joined during the weaving, leaving only one side to sew up after the foam layer was put in. If no filler is to be put in, the pad can be joined along each side during weaving, and the two sets of warp woven together at both top and bottom. Fringes can be left as trim, or the ends darned in. The foam pad can be cut to shape and placed between the warps, instead of using a paper pattern. Weave the sides closed and the cushion will be almost completed when taken from the loom.

Specifications for weaving the pad in Figures 4-3 to 4-7:

Loom: A stretcher frame, 24 in. × 26 in.

Warp: Heavy green two-ply handspun wool, 6 warps per inch. Wind the warp round and round the outside of the frame. This separates the two layers of warp so both sides can be woven.

Weft: Side 1, Figure 4-4. To weave the Ghiordes knot loops, use the same green wool as the warp and a fine two-ply Persian rug wool of green-blue. Prepare hand-hanks (butterflies) of two strands of the green wool. In some, add a strand of the green-blue, which will be used every few rows.

Side 2, Figure 4-5. The weave is countered Oriental soumak (first left to right, then return-

ing right to left). Three strands of wool are used as one weft throughout, made into hand-hanks. Use one strand each of the same green and green-blue wefts in side 1, along with one strand of very heavy yellow-green Greek goat-hair yarn.

Fig. 4-4. The looped side of the shaped chair pad.

Fig. 4-5. The Oriental soumak side of the chair pad. The heading that was woven to close the edge above the fringe shows well here. Six rows of single soumak were woven over both layers of warp. By author. (Photographs by Kent Kammerer)

There are other suitable techniques you can use. Several strands used as one weft of Greek soumak in large soft wool will produce a deep textured surface on one or both sides. At least two rows of tabby between soumak rows will firm up the weave for a still more practical cushion fabric. Sliploop or the Tibetan rug knot are also excellent technique choices. Each method goes quickly, and since the weft is used directly from the spool, no bobbins have to be prepared. These two ways go a bit better when you work on a floor loom and don't have to be concerned with the stability of the loom. A frame loom (Fig. 4-6) works best if it is fastened in a stand. With both sides woven in a deep, close pile, the soft resilient pad may not need a filler of foam for comfort.

Begin weaving the pad with six rows of single soumak, woven around all of the warps, which join the top and bottom layers to make a heading at the bottom edge of the pad, shaped to the curve of the pattern. (See Fig. 4-5.) After the single heading has been woven, weave the separate layers, for top and back.

To weave, slip the paper pattern in between the two layers of warp and begin to weave back and forth on the top layer of warp only. I started with the looped Ghiordes knot for an inch or two, then turned the frame over and began the Oriental soumak rows on the other side. (Fig. 4-7.) I found it worked well to weave some on each side, alternately, keeping the sides about even. If you prefer, you can do one whole side, then the other. Follow the shape of the paper pattern, dropping warps whenever the taper requires. These unwoven warp ends will be used to sew the sides together.

I finished the soumak side first, all the way to the top, so the paper pattern could be removed. Then I followed the shape of the soumak and finished the looped side. The soumak rows are the classic over-four-and-back-two sequence, with the rows countered—left to right, then back right to left. There are no tabby rows in between. Rows are firmly packed, but kept loose enough around the warp to make a flexible, soft surface. The turns form a neat, beaded edge.

The warps are used in pairs throughout, with two warps being woven as one (four warps per knot). Two rows of tabby are inserted between pile rows. Since no gauge except the fingers was used, a casual loop surface resulted.

For several rows above the heading, be careful to push each line of weaving down firmly, but watch that the curved bottom line does not become distorted. With a more intricate shape, you might have to weave fill-in, throw-away yarn to cover the unwoven warps and assure keeping the desired shape.

Filling and finishing are accomplished by cutting one-inch thick sheet foam slightly smaller than the paper pattern. After the weaving is removed from the loom and one side is sewn, slip the foam between the layers. Then sew the other side up to where the warp ends begin at the rounded top edge. Tie the warp end loops together in pairs, with a double knot, for a very secure seam. The loops blend into the last row of woven loops. Sewing with the warp ends which were left unwoven along the side as the weaving was tapered to shape, close the sides with an overcast stitch. All extra ends are tied and/or darned in, with any loose ends tucked inside. Because of the abrasive wear expected at the edge, I left the warp-end loops uncut. If they wear, you can always cut, plait or wrap, or just darn them in. A band edge could be made by putting loops into loops all the way across.

The fringe hanging over the edge is wider at the ends because of the curve, but wanting to leave the loops uncut, I thought it looked fine and just expressed the way it was woven.

Joanne Hall wove shaped seat cushions for two small three-legged Mexican chairs. (See Fig. C-15 in the color section.) These little chairs have personalities, and the T-shaped pads with the wide band of pattern across the widest part of the seat seem exactly right for them. The yellow pads have a pattern reminiscent of Mexican sunflowers in white, orange, and gold tones, and the colors blend with the wood of the chairs. The narrow section is in plain weave. A shape like this is woven widest part first, then the narrow length. Unwoven warp ends can be tucked into the seam that joins back to front.

Fig. 4-6. On the frame loom, the looped surface of the shaped pad in progress. Shaping has begun.

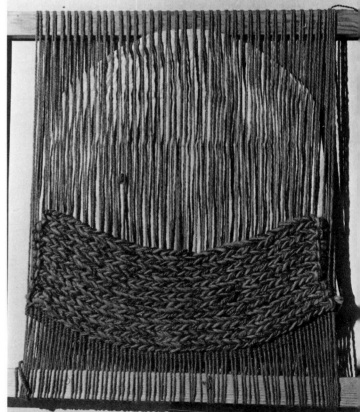

Fig. 4-7. Oriental soumak on the loom. Note the paper pattern between the warp layers. By author. (Photographs of Figs. 4-6 and 4-7 by Harold Tacker)

A tapestry that never made it to the wall is shown in Figure 4-8. It was unplanned, but when Lu Sever put it on the back of the chair, it looked so right that it stayed. A plain-weave tapestry in woodsy colors, its color, pattern, and texture harmonize with the graceful lines of the teak and suede leather chair.

This example represents another way to use your handwovens, whether they are pictorial or textures. It is kind of an updated version of the way old-time crocheted tidies, dear to the hearts of our grandmothers, were used. I wouldn't recommend this treatment for every piece of furniture, but in this case it looks appropriate.

Fig. 4-8. A rectangular Gobelin technique tapestry enhances the back of a suede chair. Woven by Luana Sever. (Photograph by Beverly Rush)

UPHOLSTERY YARDAGE

Weaving upholstery yardage gives great satisfaction and a feeling of real accomplishment when the weaving is well-designed and the furniture is enriched by your effort. This text does not deal with weaving yardage and cutting to fit, but the two fine examples of Hella Skowronski's "Leather Weave" furniture coverings should inspire you. These fabrics would perhaps be best woven in sizes and shapes to fit rather than cut to a pattern. The chair in Figure 4-9 is perfectly tailored with leather sides and fabric of woven leather strips in stripes of varied widths and colors. Figure 4-10 shows a long seat with a separate bolster back fastened to the wall. The fabric is double weave on a black and gold warp, with the black brought up at intervals between vinyl and velvet strips. The vinyl is black, red, and turquoise, and the velvet tubing is red.

Fig. 4-9. "Leather Weave" upholstery, beautifully tailored to the chair. Also notice the fine sheer casement cloth. Both textiles woven by Hella Skowronski. (Photograph by Vern Green)

Fig. 4-10. Another "Leather Weave" upholstery fabric by Hella Skowronski. This is of vinyl strips and velvet tubing.

FLAT AND PILE WEAVES IN COMBINATION

For an assortment of sound reasons, consider the flat weaves and pile weaves woven in combination for upholstery, bedspreads, or rugs. You will determine from the general idea how it works to cut down on the bulk and weight of a textile, but still retains a richly thick surface where desired. The drawing below presents the basic plan which can be adapted to other weavings and shows the shapes and their weaves within the rectangle of the warp. The sewing is simplified and a sleek fit at the corners is made easy. Eliminate a great deal of the heavy weight from a large bedspread when you want the top of the bed covered with a deep-textured fabric. For a furniture grouping where the rug is a special shape, weave flat areas extending under the furniture and perhaps for some of the walking area. Make the luxurious deep pile the feature where it will count for the most in your complete design of the group. These suggestions make good design sense and in a very practical way they permit use of less yarn without sacrificing an extravagant look. Flat weave works up faster, too, which will lessen your weaving time, if that is a factor, and the covering is nearly complete when taken off from the loom.

General directions are given for a cover for the seats of a davenport, window seat or chair, or a single cushion. Whether you weave pattern, plain, or pile weave, the overall plan and shape will be the same.

The top, back, and sides are all woven in one piece. The unwoven warp ends are cut short and darned in on one edge of the shaped corners, and the other edge is a woven selvedge, so two finished edges meet at each corner. Before starting the weaving, read the directions for the shaped pad on page 69.

Weaving Techniques

	Weaving Techniques
Seam allowance	Plain weave
Bottom	Plain or Pile weave
Side, back	Plain weave
Left and right sides	Plain or Pile weave (top)
Top	Plain weave (left and right side)
Side, front	Plain weave
Seam allowance	Plain weave

Unwoven warp at each corner

LOOM-SHAPED CUSHION COVER

Measure the piece to be covered, then make a paper or muslin pattern to check the correct size and shape.

The warp width is the maximum number of inches needed for the sides and center section plus an inch or so for weaving draw-in. The warp length should include the number of inches for seam allowance; front and back sides; top and bottom, plus allowance for weaving take-up and loom tie-in.

No exact dimensions are on the drawing as this is a general plan of procedure which can be scaled up to bedspread size or down to a small pillow cover.

First, weave the front edge of the depth of the cushion plus about 1 in. for seam allowance.

Next, weave the right and left sides plus the center section which is the top of the cushion. The sides are flat weave, and their weft continues across and back as the tabby between pile rows. Therefore, the sequence is plain weave across the full width, left to right; a row of pile knots the width of the center section only; then a row of plain weave, right to left, the full width; another row of pile weave in the center; plain weave full width left to right, and so on. Because of the heavier pile rows, the plain weave at the sides may not pack in closely, so weave in extra rows back and forth on each side width. This is the same way a selvedge is closely woven on a pile rug. Turn these extra wefts around a warp just inside of the pile weave section to avoid a slit.

When the center section and sides are woven, again narrow the weaving for the fourth plain weave side. Weave the inches required, then continue in the same width and weave the bottom, which can be plain weave, or pile weave like the top.

TO COVER AND FINISH THE CUSHION

The sewing consists of only one seam and joining the four corners. Place the cover over the form, centering the top section. Smooth out the top, folding the side pieces down, and draw the bottom section down underneath. Pin the edge of bottom and front side together. Bring the selvedges together at the corners and pin. The seams can be inconspicuously or decoratively topstitched by hand in matching yarn. This is a direct method for a smooth fit especially when a firm foam or spring cushion is being covered. However, if preferred, the corners can be sewn from the inside and the joining seam either topstitched from the outside or provided with a closure of Velcro or a zipper. The unwoven warp ends can be utilized in sewing or tying the corners. One or two warps from the tie-up length can be used to sew the seam across the width.

COLOR AND DESIGN

Weaving with the same yarns for the flat weave and on into the pile weave will unify the design. If contrasts are preferred, the flat weave can be a loom-controlled pattern—basket or plain weave—in a color to blend or contrast with the heavier surface weave. The entire cover can be a pile weave with a very short pile on the edges but deep and thick on the top surface. The design elements include: joining the corners; different weaves for sides and top; a different technique on top and bottom for a reversible cushion. You will see many more ways to use this basic idea in the design of coverings shaped in the weaving.

CHAIR CUSHION

Not woven to shape or just for this chair, Sylvia Tacker's stuffed tube pillow still nestles into the little rocking chair as if it had been. (Fig. 4-11.) The flexibility of the stuffed bands and the free warp-end pile surface of this kind of pillow make it adaptable to a chair of almost any size or shape. (See more views of this pillow in ch. 5, Figs. 5-11 and 5-12.)

Hammocks, swings, and hanging chairs are very special types of seating. They conjure up relaxed, lazy summer days, soaring through the air, dangling from a tree branch, and gentle movement. I was hoping to find some kind of hanging chair or swing and maybe a hammock, but got instead an abundance of three hammocks and three swings—including a doorway baby swing, which is in chapter 8. It begins to look like a trend—and a very exciting one. So here is another new direction to take for weavings you can use.

Fig. 4-11. Stuffed band pillow makes a soft seat pad for a little rocking chair. Weaver, Sylvia Tacker. (Photograph by Harold Tacker)

HAMMOCKS

A hammock poses an interesting problem for a weaver. It must be woven with a certain amount of "give"—but not too much stretch. It must be sturdy, but flexible, and an outdoor one, usually used in warm weather, should be airy. It should weather well. The clew and holding device must be very strong. And it helps if you have a pair of strategically placed mature trees! Following are three hammocks of diverse construction. The first one shown is an open weave, the second is of padded double weave, and the third is a flat weave, with leather trim.

I saw a lovely airy hammock that evokes visions of cool comfort on a hot summer day at the Pacific Northwest Weavers' Conference in Vancouver, B.C. (Fig. 4-12.) Shirley Medsker wove linen in a leno weave that alternates the plain weave bands with wider sections in the open weave. The strong bands of plain weave strengthen the lighter weave. Along the sides, wefts are extended, then knotted and looped for a light dancing fringe. Warp ends are knotted and drawn up for hangers at each end. Slit weave forms a band at each end for a heavy dowel to be woven through.

Figure 4-13 shows a hammock woven with a totally different approach but with as much appeal in its own way. Of padded double weave and in many colors, this reversible hammock looks secure and welcoming and comfortable. All around, fat wrapped tassels continue the wide weft strips to the outside.

Measuring 4 ft. × 9 ft., the hammock was woven by Laurie Daniells in three long sections as double-cloth tubes and stuffed during the weaving. The sections were put together with Ghiordes knots which provide a very strong join as well as the added texture of the cut ends, 4 in. long. The ends are supported by 1 in. dowels fastened to iron rings by color-coordinated wrapped sisal ropes. The warps are red and black synthetic rug yarn, set 12 e.p.i. Weft yarns in soft two- and three-ply wool and loop mohair supply a soft touch. Sometimes the colorful reversible hammock hangs on the wall with its reds, blacks, and yellows showing; other times, the side showing the subdued grays, blacks and whites is facing out. In this way the hammock is a mood-meeter as well as a comfortable place for repose.

Look up also Figure C-16 in the color section which shows the neat, tailored, and quite elegant jute and leather hammock by Marilyn Meltzer. It would be a welcome addition, in or outdoors.

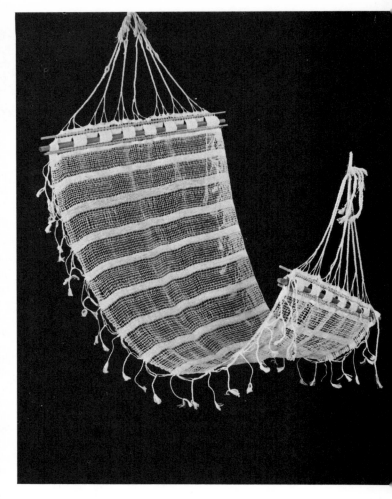

Fig. 4-12. Open leno-weave hammock with slots woven in for the spreaders. Woven by Shirley Medsker.

Fig. 4-13. Padded double-weave reversible hammock, with warm colors on one side and cool grays on the other. By weaver Laurie Daniells.

SWINGS

Innovative handwoven swings are appearing, so the idea is presented with just a few examples, to steer you in that direction. Weaving a swing is an excellent use of designing and loom skills. Fashion them in any size or shape, from a plain outdoor swing of jute with a wooden seat to an intricate indoor swing with trimmings and tassles and a shaped padded seat. The swing for a child in chapter 8 could be scaled up in size and adapted for an adult hanging chair. Use your own discretion about putting in the safety belt! Marilyn Meltzer is in the vanguard with a variety of swings, and two of hers are shown.

All of Marilyn Meltzer's swings are woven in three units: two sides and the seat. The seats are separate and padded. Each swing has a distinctive weave and trim, such as fringes, wrapped warps, pattern, and different hanging treatments.

Figure 4-14 shows an indoor swing with a subtle plaid padded seat and wide vertical bands to the ceiling. Low at each side, wrapped warps add strength and design interest and end in full tassels. The seat is plexiglass! (See also another swing by Marilyn Meltzer in Fig. C-17 of the color section.)

I have seen and heard of other swings and chairs in suspension, and maybe some particulars will give you new thoughts about seating in motion.

For the suspension, you can use wrapped rope, plaited nylon line or other strong fibers, slipcovered chain, or macrame sennits of seine twine.

Use one or two wide bands for a hanging chair or several bands joined for a hammock. A netlike stretchy hammock can be made in the sprang technique, which is basically a twisting of warps and can be combined with plain weave.

Edges can be discreet selvedges, straight fringe, knotted, plaited, scalloped fringe, added bands, or whatever you dream up.

The history of hammocks is a long one, from their origin in a pre-Columbian age, through use by navies to crowd a maximum number of crew men below decks, to present-day uses.

The netting ones are sensible beds in hot countries, and canvas is a strong fabric for other uses and climates. More than a dozen different spellings of the word have been noted. If you are interested in some hammock history and want to make one properly, there is recommended in the bibliography a small, amusing, but factual book that details how to construct different types of hammocks and how to fashion the harness or clew, which is an all-important part of the hanger at each end. Try your weaving skills and have fun producing a proper hammock and be grateful for it when you finish and need the rest!

Fig. 4-14. Indoor swing of plaid fabric with wrapped warps, tassel trim, and a plexiglass seat. Woven by Marilyn Meltzer. (Copyright pending; photograph by Marilyn Meltzer)

Chapter 5

Pillows

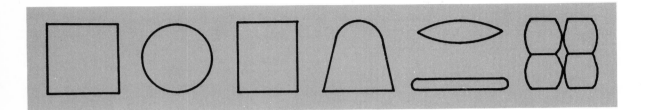

Piles of pillows can grow from your loom because you like them for color accent and comfort, or because you are a busy experimental weaver who wants and needs to explore techniques, color ways, textures, patterns, assembling, joinings, edges, and trims. (Fig. 5-1.) Weaving pillows is a perfect way to experiment in all of these directions. You can always find a use for one more pillow. If it is not too successful, it can go at the bottom of the pile or in the back row; it still is a useful object and was not a waste of effort since it has added to your knowledge of weaving. Although a pillow does not have to be large, too time-consuming, or use much yarn, you should give thought and care to the design, color, yarn, and use so that the work really will add to your skills. As long as you are sampling anyway, weave in a pillow-size. You have two sides to work with and all of those edges. I urge you to make the extra effort and weave enough for the back too. You can have a double-design project that way, and also a much handsomer reversible pillow that is a completely handwoven item. But remember that backs do show! Too many handwoven pillows have backs that are unrelated to a well-crafted top. The back can be an entirely different technique and pattern, but relate it by using the same yarns and colors as the front.

It is wise to Scotchguard the finished product before you use it.

It is fascinating to work out different ways of weaving and putting pillows together, and the more ways you try, more come tumbling along. Weaving a pillow around the pillow form is a tried and satisfactory method. Weaving both front and back around a frame loom with the warp ends used in the joining is another weaverly approach. Any time you can make the technique, the loom, and the fact of building a fabric from the warp work for you completely, you have mastered the concept and have the advantage of starting with just some yarns and a loom and creating exactly the fabric you need.

Pillows can, of course, be cut and sewn from handwoven yardage, to which you can apply innovative joinings and surface decorations, but using tools and materials to create a complete product is irresistible and a very gratifying occupation. Doing this in a useful size is just the beginning of a learning process that will show what you and your loom can accomplish. Then you can apply the concept to large-scale weavings, such as floor coverings and wall and furniture textiles. By then you will be well on your way to full use of your craft.

Fig. 5-1. A pile of pillows include fur, cut-pile wools, patterned stripes in cotton, and a patchwork of handwovens on handwoven silk/cotton. By weavers Hope Munn, Harold Tacker, Sophie Cornelison, and author. (Photograph by Harold Tacker)

Joining the seams and adding a trim opens up an entire group of other techniques and a host of ways to assemble a pillow.

Try different types of small looms while you explore. As you weave a series of pillows, see what each loom does best. A frame loom lends itself perfectly to weaving one length for front and back, or two separate pieces, on just one warping. (Fig. 5-2 and see page 120.) On a backstrap loom, weave the front and back in one length, or if you weave a tube to be stuffed, only the ends will have to be closed. Or weave a single heading at the beginning, then weave two layers, stuffing—and closing—the sides as you go. Weave another single heading to close the other end and your pillow will be finished when you cut it from the loom. Weave a tapestry pillow top on a vertical tapestry loom. Try Navaho and Salish looms, weaving those samplings into large sturdy floor pillows. Try tubular weaving on almost any loom, and fill it and use it as a bolster. Test unfamiliar loom patterns by threading your floor loom and weaving a correct pattern; then take off with adaptations, variations, and flights of fancy!

Fig. 5-2. Ring around the loom. With one warping, weave both back and front of a unit on a frame loom for a puff pillow. By author. (Photograph by Kent Kammerer)

DESIGNING A PILLOW

Some of the following ways to design and fabricate pillows may be new to you or may include a variation you had not thought of yet. A pillow does not have to be square, round, or rectangular. It is in fact a good practice exercise for a weaving that is shaped on the loom.

Draw a shape—perhaps the graceful ogee, an oval, a rectangle with rounded ends, or an uneven triangle. Any pleasing shape will do, as long as it looks right when stuffed. Work out your measurements and proportions in paper or muslin for any woven or cut pillow shape. You may want to put the filling inside the muslin, in which case your pattern will be doubly useful. I find that old pillowcases make excellent patterns and linings. Remember to allow inches all around for the thickness of the filling.

SHAPING ON THE LOOM

When you weave an original pillow shape, follow the lines of your pattern, weaving back and forth and each time turning the weft around the warp that defines the edge of the shape. The unwoven warps will be taken care of by darning in or by the joining. (See directions for weaving the shaped pad, page 69.) Make a pattern and mark the line on your warp, or place the pattern itself underneath the warp. I prefer to mark the warp with a few key dots to define the shape; then the pattern, cut from fairly stiff paper, can be laid on the weaving to check the line every few inches.

Be sure to consider which warp direction is best in relation to the edge shape as well as to any laid-in or tapestry-woven pattern. Just as in tapestry weaving, where the pattern might be woven sideways instead of vertically because of necessary interlocking, so with a pillow, an undulating edge might better be woven horizontally and molded to shape. At least think about this when you plan your weaving method and warp width. (See the shaped chair pads in Fig. C-15 of the color section and their description on p. 70.)

THE CLOSED EDGE

You may have four, three, two, one, or no open sides at all, depending upon the way you weave your cover textile:

Four seams when you use cut yardage.

Three when front and back are one length, folded around the pillow form.

Two when the weaving is tubular.

One when the tubular weaving is closed at the beginning. (See the shaped pad in ch. 4.)

And none when a tubular weaving with closed heading is stuffed as woven and the final edge closed while on the loom. Examples of these different-type closed edges follow.

CLOSURES

The joining of selvedges, warp ends, or cut edges of a pillow can be accomplished in a number of ways. Design your closing and weave the edges and ends as required. Some of the choices you have will be shown and others mentioned.

Warp end closures: These can be tied and fringed (see Fig. 5-8); tied with no fringe (directions on p. 84); loop ends chained (Fig. 5-5).

Warp and weft fringe: On both front and back sections, weave weft fringe by extending the wefts out beyond the selvedges at both sides. Allow enough length in the warp for fringe at each end, to close the edges on the pillow. Knot together the ends of back and front on all four sides. If you prefer, use the method of knotting with no fringe as given on page 84. When using cut yardage, ravel out the warp and weft for a short fringe on all sides.

Joining stitches: Use embroidery stitches for closures and the decorative stitch itself will be the join. For strength, seams can be machine- or handstitched first, then an important stitch worked over for trim.

The striped pillow in Figure 5-3 is a rectangle woven of unspun wool on a wool warp and wrapped around a box-pillow form. The selvedges are sewn together down each side with orange yarn to match the warp. The two ends slightly overlapping about a third of the way down the face of the pillow instead of joining along the top edge are a functional and decorative feature. Five-strand joining secures the seam and covers it well. Thick unspun wool is used to complement the pillow fabric and is caught down with the same orange yarns used in the warp. Because four of the strands are not sewn through the fabric, many strands and the thick unspun wool can be used. The catch stitch is made with just one strand of yarn; it is the single dark line in the photograph. The ends were worked into two large rings, with thick short tassels continuing from the band.

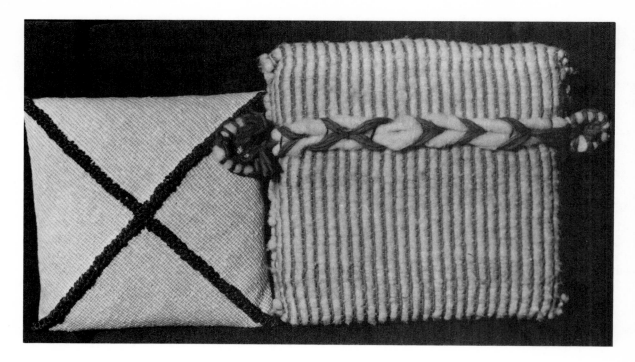

Fig. 5-3. Two square pillows, each made with one piece of fabric. Left: a square with corners brought to the center, around a knife-edge pillow form. Seams are joined with Sorbello embroidery stitch in heavy wool yarn. Right: unspun wool woven into a rectangle and wrapped around a box pillow form. The seam is caught together with 5-strand joining of unspun wool and worsted yarn. (Photograph by Harold Tacker)

The five-strand joining looks much more complicated than it is, and is quite simple to do once you learn the steps. Because it is both useful and versatile, directions and illustrations are given to help you. After you learn the procedure, vary it in any number of ways. The joining can be very showy and dominating or matching and narrow. The catch stitch sews the seam, but if more strength is needed or the stitches are far apart, the seam can be sewn first by hand or machine and the joining yarns will cover it. Either or both ends of the strands can be darned in out of sight or made important with wrapping or knotting. The catch thread has to be smooth and fine enough to sew through the cloth easily, but the laid-on yarns can be just as bulky as you wish. Color arrangements are almost endless, as each of the five strands may be a different color. Study the photographs of this joining in Figures 5-3 and 5-4. Follow the directions, and I think you will be pleased to add this joining to your store of finishing techniques.

Fig. 5-4. An expanded example of the five-strand joining shows the path taken by each of the strands. (Photograph by Harold Tacker)

HOW TO DO THE FIVE-STRAND JOINING

Bring the two pieces of your cloth together, either just touching or overlapped. Pin or overcast with a long basting stitch to hold the seam together. The basting stitches can be removed later, if they are not covered. Anchor the cloth to the table in some way so both hands are free to sew. Follow the yarn path in Figure 5-4 and the drawing at right and proceed:

Strand 1 (the sewing thread) is threaded into a needle and will fasten down the four strands.

Bring 1 up at a, over strands 3 and 4, and down at b, making a straight top stitch to sew the two strands down.

Move 3 and 4 out to the sides, and bring strands 2 and 5 in to the center and catch them down with strand 1, which comes up at c and down at d.

Move 2 and 5 out to the sides and bring 3 and 4 back to the center. Repeat the catch stitch and continue alternating the pairs of strands.

When you become proficient in the method, you can design some quite elaborate versions with different catch stitches and change the order of crossing the strands. Notice the strand-crossing variation on the unspun wool pillow.

The large pillow in Figure 5-5 was woven with fat unspun wool-chenille and large Mexican wool yarn. Made in one piece on a frame loom, with loop warp ends, it is really a continuous circle with two open selvedges. It was woven on two sides of the loom, just as with the shaped pad (Fig. 4-3) and Dawn's play-pillow (Fig. 8-12). The frame was taken apart, and the loop warps were chained together for the closure, which is shown in Figure 5-5. When you weave a pillow like this, leave two or three inches of unwoven warp at each end of the weaving, as you weave first on one side of the loom and then the other. Two different patterns were woven, but using the same yarns for both. (Figs. 5-6 and 5-7.) When you are finished, pull the frame apart at the corners and slip off the continuous ring of weaving. Sew up one side and stuff the pillow with dacron batting or insert a pillow form; then sew up the other side. Use your finger as a crochet hook and chain the warp loops across one end, then across the other. Fasten a tassel or some other treatment to the corners, incorporating the last loop of the chain.

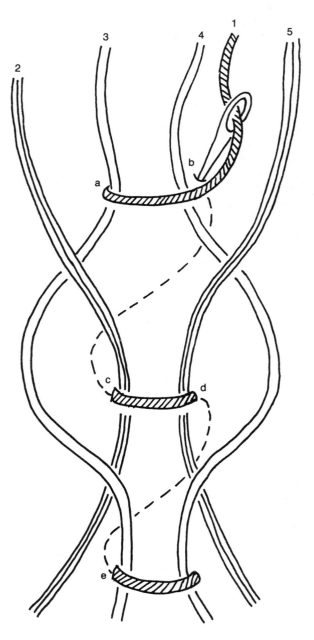

FIVE-STRAND JOINING

82

Fig. 5-5. The chained warp loop closing across the end of the Big Chenille pillow is shown. The same closing is used across the other end.

Fig. 5-6. One side of the Big Chenille pillow is woven in basket weave and Greek and Oriental soumak.

Fig. 5-7. Reverse side of the Big Chenille pillow. The chained warp loop closing and tied ends show at the top.

83

CUT END CLOSINGS

The pillow on the right in Figure 5-8 is a long rectangle and was in fact made from part of a long, wide sampling of white raw silk and spun and unspun wools. Two consecutive sections, all in the same yarns but with slightly different patterns, were used to wrap around the pillow form. The selvedges were smoothly sewn with matching yarn and the cut warp ends tied. Figure 5-9 shows quite clearly the row of knots with the ends spreading out from them. This treatment is most effective when the warp is of interesting spins and colors and closely set. This warp is several sizes of silk and wool in several shades of white.

To do the closing shown in Figure 5-9, the cloth should be just the length needed to go around the pillow form and meet exactly where the warp ends will be tied. If you use batting, you can make the pillow fit your cloth. If you use a molded pillow form and your cloth is too long, you can ravel out a few rows before making the ties, so the pillow will be smooth. Start at one corner and tie two or three pairs of warp from the two ends of cloth. Then tie one or two at the other corner, to bring the cloth up in place, and continue from the first corner. I find it handy to place the pillow between my knees, so I can hold the edges and pillow firm and have both hands free to do a smooth knotted row. Just tie a double knot, bringing the ends out at each side. In use, the ends may shake into a full fringe, which also looks fine, like a ruff.

For a knotted seam with no fringe, follow the same directions but after each knotted group, bring the ends toward you and between the two edges of cloth. The next knot is tied over and the ends are tucked inside. Continue in this way, tucking the final ends back inside. You can do as I did in Dawn's pillow. (See Fig. 5-14.) Because the warp ends were quite long, I had an accumulated bunch at the corner which I wrapped and left in a tassel "handle." One tassel was formed on a corner of each two units. So there are two handles on opposite corners at one end of the pillow.

A row of small knots makes a nice seam, and in a deep pile or textured weave it is almost invisible.

VARIATIONS ON A SQUARE

Weave one large square to make a complete pillow with line design on the top, a plain surface on the back—and no joined edges on any of the four sides. (See Fig. 5-3, at left.) With no seams along the edges, the pillow takes a lot of hard use and stays in shape. Weave the exact size you need or cut it from a woven length. The latter is simple to do, but because the square is the whole pillow cover—back and front—be sure to try the size out in muslin first, to be certain that your square is large enough. It is easiest to work with a molded pillow form in this case.

To assemble this pillow, place a square pillow form on the square of fabric, so the corners of the pillow are in the center of each side of the fabric and the corners of the cloth form equal triangles. Pull the corners of fabric to the center of the pillow until the tips of the triangles just meet. Pin them and if necessary, to hold them in place, sew a long overcast stitch along each seam which can be removed after the join is made, or be covered and remain. Topstitch with the decorative embroidery stitch of your choice and your pillow is complete. I used the Sorbello stitch in heavy handspun wool of a darker shade than the light beige of the hand-loomed tweed. Herringbone, closed cross stitch, or chevron stitch would also be satisfactory joinings for this kind of pillow.

There are lots of design possibilities in a project like this: try working out a striped arrangement or plan colors in warp and weft for a colorful tied fringe joining.

The seam lines quite naturally will extend out into some kind of corner embellishment also —and can be knotted or tasseled, or wrapped. Embroidery stitches could also be added in and around the seam joining.

The large square could be made up like a patchwork and put together in the same way—but the whole point of this project is the simplicity of only one square of cloth, joined only on the top.

HOW TO AVOID SEWING A PILLOW COVER

It is possible to weave the pillow covering right on the pillow, by winding warp around the foam pillow form and using a tapestry needle as the shuttle, Oriental and Greek soumak work very well for this method, with or without rows of plain weave between. Be sure to pack the rows in very, *very* closely since pillows take a lot of handling and punching and yarn too loosely woven spreads to show the form beneath. I have found that Ghiordes knot works very well for this kind of weaving, with either plain weave or soumak rows between.

It is somewhat better working over a knite- or rounded-edge pillow form than over a boxed form, where you have to put another warp around to weave the sides. Covering a round form is very satisfactory, also; warp so that the yarn spokes out from the center.

All of the methods of finishing, closing, and assembling that have been described apply to working with cut squares or rectangles. The sides can be sewn by hand, stitched, and covered with a fancy stitch, or raveled out to provide ends for tying. At the left of Figure 5-8 is a pillow made from odds and ends from the sample and leftover boxes. An old but always good idea is to make patchwork patterns on a handwoven background, or to construct the whole thing from scraps. Figure 5-8 shows one side, Figure 5-17 the other. The background, both back and front, is woven of white raw silk over a dark, mixed warp of two blues, very dark red, and gold color. The seams were sewn by hand with thread in a matching blue, the warps and wefts were raveled out along each side to give two colors of fringe—an excellent design idea to plan. Each side of the pillow was first appliquéd with pieces of handwoven material. The pieces are all in the same jade and Chinese blue and off-white range since they were samplings made for upholstery to go on a chair beside a Chinese jade lamp. The pieces were moved about until I was pleased with the composition, then sewn on invisibly. Some patches are fringed.

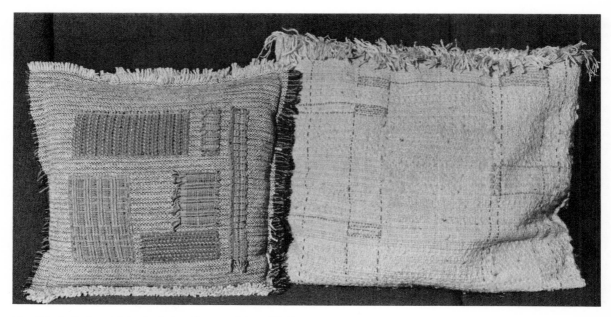

Fig. 5-8. Left: A patchwork of sampling swatches. Right: One long rectangle wrapped around a soft pillow form of dacron batting, with warp ends tied at the top for a closing and trim.

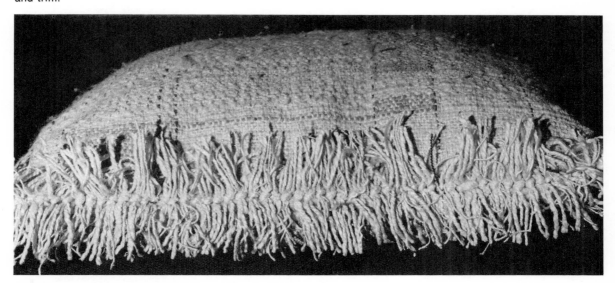

Fig. 5-9. The closed edge of the white pillow shows the even row of knots that join the two edges and provide a fringe. Figs. 5-3 and 5-5 to 5-9 by author. (Photographs of Figs. 5-5 to 5-9 by Harold Tacker)

BAND PILLOWS

Woven bands as both warp and weft are interwoven to cover front and back of the pillow in Figure 5-10. Weave the bands around the pillow form. Fasten all of the warp ends at one side and leave a row of short warp fringe. These bands were all woven in the same pattern with the same red-orange, red, and blue yarns, but they are not identical in the placement of the colors. Thus, the bands have a uniform look, but the interest of a subtle variation. There is a wealth of color and pattern variety possible and a good use of sturdy woven bands in a pillow like this.

Sew bands into tubes, fill them with dacron batting, then assemble them into pillows and chair pads, or expand them into a beach or pool lounging pad. Try a padded band pillow as a back and seat cushioning for a wooden rocking chair. (See Fig. 4-11.) Plop one on a slat or plastic-woven chaise lounge for more comfort. Contour a chair pad with thick and thin and wide and narrow bands to conform to the figure. Weave bands of different widths and combine them to fit the situation. Each band can have a subtle color variation, for example, plain bright colors will make bold stripes. Use the warp ends and selvedge edges as part of your texture and design. Once you begin with band ideas, the possibilities multiply so fast you won't be able to carry out all of them.

Sylvia Tacker made the soft fluffy chair pillow in Figures 5-11 and 5-12 especially for this book. (The pillow was also photographed in her childhood rocker in Fig. 4-11.) Pillows made from padded bands are flexible and useful. When woven of soft acrylic yarns and stuffed with dacron, they are very practical too, because they can be washed successfully. The Tackers made pads—each one a different band pattern—for their teak dining room chairs.

Fig. 5-10. Band pillow. Interwoven bands cover the back and front of a pillow, with ends left in a warp fringe. (Photograph by Harold Tacker)

The bands for the padded band pillow were woven on a special band loom devised by Harold Tacker, but bands can be woven on any type loom. Warp ends were left about three inches long for trim at each end of the bands. One pair of bands was sewn together down each side with an overcast stitch in matching yarn. Dacron batting was packed in lightly. For even distribution, fill the tube as you go—sew a few inches, then stuff, sew and stuff—until it is nicely rounded; then finish the seams. Line up the stuffed bands, use the warp ends as spots of pile weave, and join any number of tubes for the size pillow you need. In this pillow, which is in grays, black, and white, the tubes are of different lengths so that the fluffy warp ends punctuate the weaving at random. Another way to achieve texture and pattern in a band pillow is shown in Figure 5-13. Wide, flat joining stitches provide another possible design element. You can combine unpadded and padded tubes, using the padding just at comfort points and doing the rest in flat weaving.

Fig. 5-11. Top side of a padded band pillow, with warp end fringes.

Fig. 5-12. The other side of the padded band pillow.

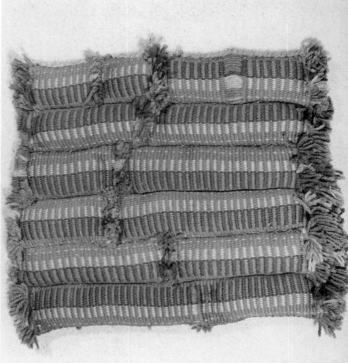

Fig. 5-13. Another band pillow, with different pattern and fewer fringes. Note the unwoven warp in the top right-hand band. This is how the random fringes occur. The ends are sewn together and the unwoven warp is cut or left as loops. Pillows in Figures 5-10 to 5-13 by Harold and Sylvia Tacker.

PUFF PILLOW IN UNITS

Dawn's puff play-pillow (Fig. 5-14) is described in detail in chapter 8, but you can use the same directions to make a large-scale floor pillow of stuffed units. Just use a larger frame, larger-size yarn, and weave Oriental or Greek soumak, which gives a raised spongy surface and adds depth and softness. Each unit could be a foot or more square, with as many units joined as you want. Make rectangles, if that suits your purpose. A thick raised pile for part of the pattern will add still more interest and comfort. Colors can be bold and fearless! Fill each unit really full of dacron batting to make the cushion plump. Make your flat sections plenty large because when they are stuffed and rounded, the overall measurements will be several inches smaller. For a finished pillow about 24 in. square on the floor, make each of the four units at least 15 in. square. When you put in three or more inches of batting, several inches of your flat measurement puffs up into the air! If you are using some kind of lapped joining, allow extra for that too, but there is no need for extra inches if the units are just touching. If your units do seem too small at this point, join them with a wide stitch or put them together with stuffed or flat woven bands. It is wise to experiment with sizes; try out your pillow ideas with muslin over batting or pillow forms to be very sure your weaving will be the size you expect.

Aves Pickering combined weaving and sprang in a decorative wool pillow. (Fig. 5-15.) The background is a flat weave, and light sprang warps are woven in at the top and bottom. For the overlay, the sprang warps are twisted as a top layer above the weaving. Tassels of the light yarn are fastened to each corner. The back of the pillow is in the same flat weave as the front.

Fig. 5-14. Dawn's Puff Pillow is a longish rectangle floor pillow for a young lady to sit or lie upon, or play with. Four units were woven, stuffed, and joined. By author. See also Figures 8-11 and 8-12. (Photographs of Figs. 5-11 to 5-14 by Harold Tacker)

Fig. 5-15. Sprang and weaving are combined for a pillow covering. Aves Pickering, weaver. (Photograph by William Eng)

Montezuma's emblem, sometimes depicted in Aztec Indian lore in green and gold feathers, was the design inspiration for the plump pillow in Figure 5-16. Lila Winn wove her own version of the Ghiordes knot to achieve a slightly raised texture, but not a true pile weave. Although the knot was worked in the circle with a continuous weft, no loops were raised. The pulled-down flat loop makes a smooth surface, but with more texture than that of the plain weave around the central design. Filled with shredded foam, the pillow was made entirely of handspun wool in traditional colors—off-white, gray-green, and soft gold. A tightly plaited cord of natural dark gray wool trims the edge.

Fig. 5-16. The round medallion woven on a square pillow of handspun wool represents Montezuma's emblem. By weaver Lila Winn. (Photograph by Kent Kammerer)

"BONUS-WARP" PILLOWS

Weavers are notably ingenious (and thrifty); they use up every scrap of fabric and every last thrum in trims or other ways. Jan Burhen wove pillows on the warps left unwoven along each side of a burnoose hood. (See Fig. C-18 in the color section.) After weaving two pieces like this, put them together for pillows, and accent the warp stripes by bringing the long thrums up to the top surface. Work them into braids with tasseled ends, catching them down to the pillow fabric with a few stitches. *Voila!* Free pillows!

Karen Kaufman wisely tries out various techniques, yarns, and use of fur strips by weaving big pillows. As a study while planning a rug to be woven in the old Norwegian *Krokbragd* method, she did several pillows, some with patterned stripes in bright colors and one with a simple zigzag pattern and wide bands of woven strips of fur, woven on three harnesses. *Krokbragd* means "crooked path," and the technique resembles just that. Single- or double-point threading on three, four, or six harnesses produces unlimited small patterns created by the color changes. Traditionally, just three colors were used. The technique is excellent for pile rugs, since it provides a plain-weave ground and the opportunity for weaving a patterned heading. For flat-weave rugs, the tightly packed weft makes a thick, soft pad, with reversible pattern.

Five quite dissimilar but fairly harmonious pillows that were lined up for their photograph in Figure 5-17 point up the fact that a whole pile of handwoven pillows somehow looks right. From the left: the Big Chenille described earlier; Harold Tacker's pile weave pillow woven in two strips that were invisibly joined; a pillow woven by Hope Munn, who used strips of almost-black soft fur and rich orange-red suede leather for an appealingly soft cushion; the other side of the blue patchwork pillow shown in Figure 5-8 in which patches cover all of the ground fabric except for the light square and a narrow border; and a pillow with stripes woven in fine mercerized cotton in blended shades of yellow, light brown, and orange. This last pillow is one of a long series woven by Sophie Cornelison, who has great success threading her loom to small patterns, then weaving many variations in treadling and color combinations for small pillows and large floor cushions.

Fig. 5-17. Pillows in a row. Chenille, cut pile, fur and suede, handwoven patches, and pattern stripes. (Photograph by Harold Tacker)

A truly big floor pillow, 4 ft. × 3 ft., was woven by Barbara O'Steen. (Fig. 5-18.) The plain-weave tapestry technique flows and models into color changes and shapes, with added loops and cut pile. The colors are warm tones of gold and yellow and white merging into browns, in yarns of different weights. The back is soft golden suede leather.

Suede strips alternate with woven wool bands on Kerstin Schweizer's trimly tailored hassock. (Fig. 5-19.) The woven pattern of each band across the top is the same, but different colors or combinations of the same colors were used. The leather and bands are in rich rust, orange, gold, dark green, and brown. The cover closes with a zipper, and the bottom is of suede. The sides are girded with an unpat-terned band.

These are a mere selection from the vast possibilities. Enter the realm of pillow weaving for the excitement of trying new and different techniques and color ways.

Fig. 5-18. A big floor pillow, about 4 ft. × 3 ft., in tapestry and pile weaves, with a suede leather back. By weaver Barbara O'Steen. (Photograph by Harold Tacker)

Fig. 5-19. Hassock of woven wool bands and suede leather. In green, brown, and a range of autumn colors. By weaver Kerstin Schweizer. (Photograph by Harold Tacker)

Chapter 6

Bed Coverings

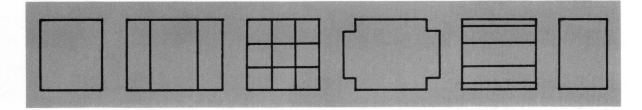

At this writing, quilts are "in"—as art forms and for use. Old techniques are being rediscovered, and bed covers are being woven, quilted, stuffed, patchworked, and embroidered —sometimes all of these in one production. The textile cycle has turned again and come around to the spreads, quilts, and blankets that were so much part of doweries and necessary household possessions in early days. Weaving bed sheets and coverlets was part of a future housewife's daily learning. And making quilts was a sociable pastime as well as a useful occupation that satisfied the Puritan ethic. The very word "comforter" has a cozy, warm connotation. (Fig. 6-1.) What better way to express comfort than with a soft wool covering, padded and puffed for warmth and softness? It is interesting to speculate why—in this age of electric blankets—the creative urge has turned to this expression. Maybe new textile craftsmen, having learned skills and techniques and put the results of their learning on the wall, where the only practical requirement is that they will stay there, have now applied their experience to useful household textiles. A bed cover has to be within a size limit and has to be well-made to withstand lifting, folding, and cleaning. It is as exciting a design problem as a wall decoration, but goes beyond it into real usefulness. Craftsmen are "thinking big." Quilts and spreads are good subjects for assembling strips or pieces. In this chapter, some of the ways to assemble a bed cover will be described.

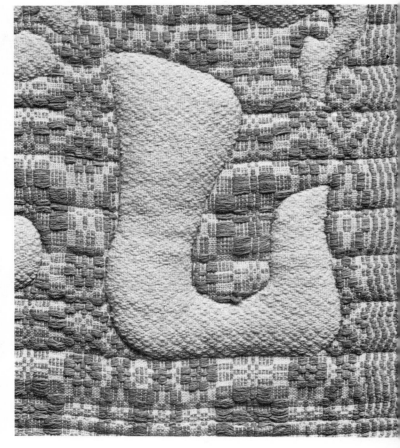

Fig. 6-1. Detail of Luana Sever's "Old Colonial Comforter," better known as the "Love Quilt." (Photographs of Figs. 6-1 to 6-16 by Beverly Rush)

TRADITIONAL PATTERN

Remember the lovely old coverlet patterns when you plan a bed cover. Do as Ethel Jackson did: She adapted Dornik weave pattern repeats to her widths, but made them pink and white instead of the traditional indigo or brown; and she added a handmade fringe. Loom patterns in rows of plain and pattern weave serve your design as borders, stripes, or patches of pattern on plain weave. Try weaving the pattern in a contrasting color with some of the pattern in the background color for a subtle color/pattern play. A nostalgic look is beautifully combined with a modern use of color and pattern in the Love Quilt. (Fig. 6-1.) An updated use of pattern might be a combination of overscaled and very much smaller-scale pattern blocks. Try the previously mentioned suggestion of adding some surface texture—loops, for instance—around or within the pattern. This would be very effective on a bedspread. Blow up one pattern unit to bed-size, weaving

it in laid-in or tapestry technique. (See "Big Twills," Fig. 3-5.)

Ethel Jackson wove her bedspread in a classic loom-controlled pattern, the Rose in Dornik weave. (Figs. 6-2 and 6-3.) Even the color is appropriate—pink and off-white! The warp and ground weft are a natural unbleached Egyptian cotton. The pattern weft is pink mercerized cotton and is also used for the fringe, which puts just the right finishing edge on the spread. Four squares instead of the traditional five are repeated to make the pattern come out even in the necessary widths. Three lengths are joined and so carefully matched that it is difficult to see where the joining is. Looped fringe was woven with several skeleton warps, which were later removed, to leave a full fringe. The spread is beautifully handcrafted throughout—the planning, the weaving, and the finishing—by a very fine experienced weaver.

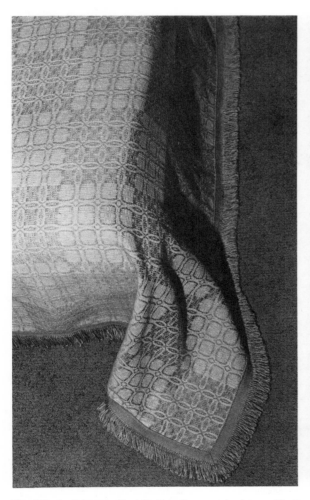

Fig. 6-2. A pink and off-white Dornik weave bedspread has three strips joined. Handwoven fringe is applied all around the edge. Woven by Ethel Jackson.

Fig. 6-3. A detail of the Dornik weave bedspread shows the perfect handwoven fringe edging.

There must have been a twinkle in her eye when Luana Sever named the quilt in Figures 6-1 and 6-4 "Old Colonial Comforter"! (See also Fig. C-8 in the color section.) The colonial weavers of indigo coverlets must be doing some tossing and turning! Four pieces, all in wool yarns, were woven in double weave in a traditional loom-controlled pattern and stuffed with dacron as they were woven. Pattern and color are very well thought out and the word "Love" is quilted in large rounded letters. The orange and fuchsia colors are very much of today.

Fig. 6-4. The "Love Quilt" is double woven, padded, and quilted. Woven in four pieces and joined. By Luana Severs.

TACOMA WEAVERS' GUILD TAPESTRY BEDSPREAD

Members of the Tacoma, Washington, Weavers' Guild combined their time and talents to create a very handsome bedspread. (Figs. 6-5 to 6-16, 8-4 to 8-7, and C-20 and C-21 in the color pages.) This was their Guild display at the Pacific Northwest Handweavers Conference in Portland, Oregon, and they received the top award for it. The whole idea was so intriguing and the finished product so excellent that photographs of almost all of the individual tapestries, as well as views of the back showing the quilting and the way the spread looks on the bed, have been included. Twenty members wove the square tapestries; one member wove the joining yardage; and other members helped in the assembling and quilting. An interesting sidelight is that the weaving skills and experience ranged from beginners weaving a first tapestry to the expertise of long-time, award-winning weaver-designers.

Fig. 6-5. The Tacoma Weavers' Guild tapestry bedspread. Some of the individual tapestries in the bedspread, woven by different members of the Guild, are shown in Figures 6-6 through 6-14. Courtesy of Dr. and Mrs. Eugene V. Lagerberg.

A brief summary of the main elements of the project follows.

Weaving requirements: Twenty plain-weave tapestry squares, all the same size.

Individual designs: The weaver chose any subject from nature.

Yarn and pattern colors: Wool in clear, strong colors.

Tapestry backgrounds: All of the same homespun natural white wool.

Joining: Squares were to be joined by strips of handwoven homespun natural white wool. A border of the same fabric was used all around.

Finishing: The back was to be of off-white fabric, filled with a dacron batt, and then quilted by hand.

Assembling: All tapestry squares, the border material, and the back yardage were washed and shrunk before putting the spread together.

The finished tapestries were laid out and shuffled about until a pleasing arrangement was found. The patterned squares were sewn to the joining strips for the top.

Top: Tapestries sewn together with border and joining strips.

Middle: Dacron quilt batt.

Bottom: Fine off-white slub linen yardage that looks handwoven was purchased for the back fabric.

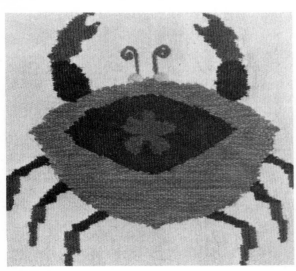

Fig. 6-6. Crab.

Fig. 6-8. Owl.

Fig. 6-7. Butterfly.

Fig. 6-9. Fresh fruit.

98

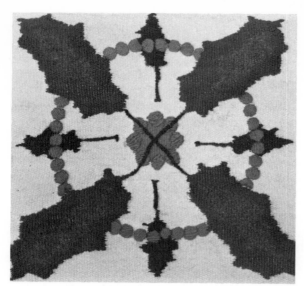

Fig. 6-10. Holly berries and leaves.

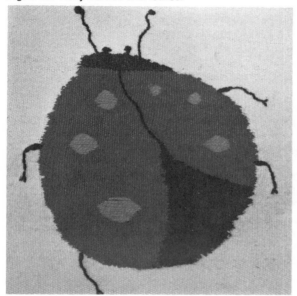

Fig. 6-11. Ladybug.

Fig. 6-13. Sheep and bird-in-a-tree.

Fig. 6-12. Snail.

Fig. 6-14. A one-apple tree.

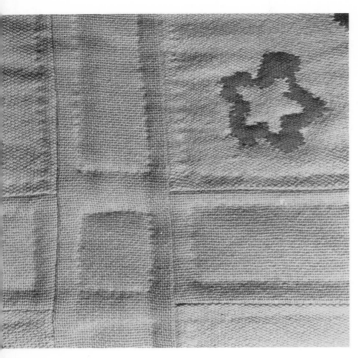

Fig. 6-15. Detail of joining strips and quilting in the tapestry bedspread.

The assembled layers were put on a quilting frame. Small quilting bees of two to four weavers at a time worked at quilting by hand around each tapestry pattern. (Fig. 6-15.) Rows and squares in a subtle block pattern were quilted on the joining pieces with very neat mitered corner seams. (Fig. 6-16.) The bedspread's reverse side bears an attractive line design of each pattern. The good craftsmanship would make it possible to use the quilt "wrong-side" up! A project like this involves an incalculable number of hours, but a weaver could do it as a long-term labor of love, and perhaps involve some family members to help create a family heirloom.

Karen Kaufman used imagination and weaving knowledge in fabricating two bed coverings, decidedly different in method, colors, and appearance. Each is an excellent example of weaving in units to produce a large textile on a small loom.

The tapestry blanket with fur shown in Figure 6-17 is composed of three rectangles, each 18 in. wide and 6 ft. long, woven on a warp of soft wool. The weft is Swedish wool and strips of fur. Since the seams are invisible, the blanket is reversible—appearing the same on both sides. The fur was twisted into small tubes so the hairs stick out on both sides, and of course the plain weave tapestry is the same. Working from a sketch, Karen thought of hills and mountains and blended subtle muted colors in a pattern that continues and flows across the three panels. The softness of the fur and wool and the quiet colors make this blanket look warm and inviting.

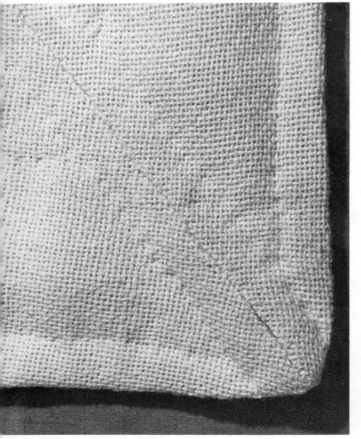

Fig. 6-16. A neatly mitered corner of the tapestry bedspread.

Fig. 6-17. Fur and tapestry-weave reversible blanket, woven in three rectangles. By weaver Karen Kaufman. (Photograph by Karen Kaufman)

The quilt in Figure 6-18 also looks warm. (See also Fig. C-22 in the color section.) The name given the cover is "Red Quilt," but it has a color range from yellow- and red-orange to red, pink, fuchsia, purple, and bright blue. The warps and wefts change from different color crossings. The strips were all woven with Swedish wool on a table loom, then assembled into four sections which are joined by card-woven bands. The bands, woven in an ogee pattern, are in some of the same colors as the fabric. Chainstitch covers some of the joinings.

Each of the quilt's four sections is composed of three strips—two 16 in. wide and one 8 in. wide—which were sewn together. The card-woven patterned bands extend the measurements and the finished quilt is about 84 in. wide by 106 in. long. There is quilting around the various color blocks, with some embroidery added at the joinings. Where the four bands meet, long warp fringes hang free for a natural center of interest. (Fig. 6-19.)

To weave and live with an oversized bedspread and make it a manageable size requires some special planning. If your loom is a small one, even more thought must be put on the problem. One way to solve it is to weave two, three, or four sections and zip them together. The very narrow zippers will be inconspicuous, or Velcro can be applied and the seams should be a part of the total design.

If it isn't necessary to take the sections apart very frequently, the joinings can be made with the plan of removing the stitches when necessary and then rejoining them. Think about the idea of using three strips, with two lighter-weight lengths for the sides and a heavy one for the center which would lap over several inches and keep the edge pieces in place with no actual joining. Then each of the three pieces can be removed and folded separately.

Adapt the plan shown in the drawing on p. 74 and leave the corners unwoven to save bulk and weight and to achieve smooth corners whether the spread hangs to the floor or is tucked in all around.

Fig. 6-18. "Red Quilt," woven in four sections and joined with card-woven bands.

Fig. 6-19. A close-up detail shows where the joining bands meet in the "Red Quilt." By Karen Kaufman. (Photographs of Figs. 6-18 and 6-19 by Harold Tacker)

AFGHANS

Throws, afghans, nap-robes, knee-robes. Call them what you will, they are useful and comforting weavings to have around. They give you a chance to do some fine weaving with colorful or subtle luxuriously soft wools and mohair yarns. Make them as small as a knee-warmer or as large as a bed. Edges can be bound with soft leather or wool; you can use an embroidered edge stitch, woven bands, long knotted fringe, short straight fringe, or any edge that is appropriate to the weaving. Weave plaids, stripes, or loom patterns. Weave and join squares and rectangles. Afghans represent a fine opportunity to let your imagination run free so that you can weave with few restrictions and great originality.

The three afghans in Figure 6-20 are equally soft but of quite different yarns and weaves. From left: Subtle stripes in autumn tones, woven in featherweight brushed wool; the end finish is a short straight fringe. Next, white unspun wool with a laid-in pattern of unspun madrona-dyed wool, has a plain hem. Then a twill weave—which is an excellent choice for weaving a soft, supple textile—in Finnish loop mohair and brushed wool, with a broad-striped plaid pattern in warm gold and orange, with long fringe simply knotted.

Fig. 6-20. Three soft afghans. From left to right: brushed wool from Ireland; unspun wool, by author; mohair and brushed wool, by Sylvia Tacker. (Photograph by Harold Tacker)

HEADBOARDS

Weaving a headboard for a wide or narrow bed is an interesting design and use project for a weaver. Fabric can be woven to size and shape, then framed. Or your textile can be stretched over a frame. You can quilt it, pad it, or weave it in high and low textures, or simply design it to be hung on the wall to look like a part of the bed. Coordinate the bedspread for a unified, designed look by weaving the spread in the same yarns and colors as the headboard.

Naomi Everett wove a "headboard" to hang on the wall from a brass curtain rod. (Fig. 6-21.) The fabric is of stripes and open weaves, in red and white. The wide red wool herringbone stripes have a narrow band of very pale yellow on either side. The white sections are of nubby linen. Brooks Bouquet provides lacelike areas, and unwoven warps, alternated with open spaced warp, create an interesting pattern of rectangles. The red wool warps extend several inches below the woven cloth and end in tied tassels. A large lead fishing weight hidden in each long tassel helps the panel hang well and stay in place.

Another type of headboard for fastening to the wall is shown in Figure 6-22. The subject of this project was a carved pile weave, with some padding, woven with heavy wool yarns to have an architectural look. Color, depth of pile, and yarns for the two patterns were explored to see which would create the desired effects and lend themselves to the different techniques used. The depths and levels were achieved by these techniques: plain weave for the lowest level, Oriental and Greek soumak for two somewhat higher surfaces, and Ghiordes knot pile for the highest carved areas which are rounded and tapered. Dacron batting pads some of the pattern at the left.

The design source for this study is the time-weathered carving on Irish high crosses. As an aid to the use of light and dark yarns, color, and in the clipping, it is helpful to study photographs and actual relief carvings, to see where the shadows and highlights fall. Proceed cautiously at first, so that you don't clip off all of your carefully woven pile, all the way down to the collar of the knot! When you start a sheared weaving, do some clipping after about three or four inches of knotting to make sure the pile is the length needed for the depth wanted.

Thereafter you can weave a whole section before you go back to snipping and contouring. Use very sharp scissors, sharp all the way to the tips. Snip, pat, and brush. When you are finished, a gentle vacuuming or brushing will remove all fine clippings and freshen the color. Since the surface of this kind of weaving is pushed about as you work, you will have to groom it when you finish. (See also the section on carved pile in ch. 2 for more information about this technique and the Ghiordes knot variation which gains more wefts per inch in the drawing, p. 39.)

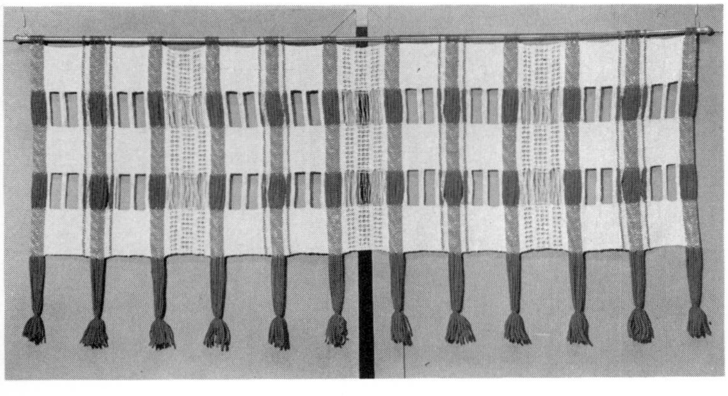

Fig. 6-21. A headboard created from a woven panel hung on a brass rod. In red wool and white linen. Woven by Naomi Everett. (Photograph by Harold Tacker)

Fig. 6-22. Study for a carved pile woven headboard in various wools and techniques. By author. (Photograph by Harold Tacker)

Chapter 7

Table Textiles

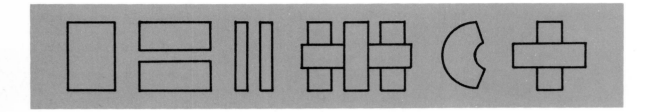

A great deal has been written and said about beautiful handwoven tablecloths and place mats, for there is nothing so luxurious and lovely as a table dressed in handwoven linen. (Fig. 7-1.) Place mats woven in every kind of yarn and fiber, in familiar loom-patterns, and planned to coordinate with dishes and silver are always a pleasure to use, to see, and to weave. Obliged to select a very few table textiles only, I decided to stick to the overall plan of the text and suggest some ideas for using strips, units, and shaped weaving.

SAMPLER RUNNERS

Looking through Ethel Jackson's box of sampling strips—the results of workshops and of her own experimenting with loom patterns and variations—a thought struck me: Why not plan your samplings for color and size and use them for table runners?

Weave your handwoven runners over and under on your table to provide the settings you need, and each time do it a different way. Your linens will fit any size table, whether it is round or square. The arrangement can be adjusted for two, four, or more settings.

Fig. 7-1. Red and white place mat woven in a Sea Star
pattern. (Place mat, combined with runners, is also in Fig.
7-7.) By Ethel Jackson.

The next thought was to use samplers already woven. Mrs. Jackson obligingly let me borrow hers, and Beverly Rush and I arranged, photographed, and rearranged them. We came up with some workable ways to cover a round table, as well as a number of arrangements that worked on rectangular tables. (Figs. 7-2, 7-3, and 7-4.) The results were surprisingly effective, even with these unplanned colors and pattern weaves. The idea works well. What fun it would be to do this for a weavers' luncheon, and what conversation and discussion of weaves would result! Even when used this way, your samplers will be just as available for reference; you can label or number them on the back.

Fig. 7-3. 8-harness reverse twill and 8-harness twill woven in black and white. A black line down the center separates the two styles of threading. This is a way of weaving a great number of sampling variations, and the division provides an interesting design element.

Fig. 7-2. Sampler runners woven over and under on a round table.

Fig. 7-4. Three runners in a row, for two place settings opposite each other on a round table. There are one narrow strip and two wider ones. Runners in Figs. 7-2 to 7-4 all woven by Ethel Jackson. (Photographs by Beverly Rush)

PLANNED STRIPS

Interweave the strips for a new table setting every time, right on the table. Weave different widths and lengths. Weave fine ones for indoor use and rugged ones for outdoor terrace or deck tables. Select colors that will be harmonious with your room and dishes and with each other to give you a wide choice in assembling them. Figures 7-5 and C-19 in the color section show bright yellow linen strips woven for the purpose of combining with other weavings in various ways. The heavy linen plain weave is bordered with a white pattern. A pair of gray linen runners with the same white border is being woven to add more variety to the possible arrangements.

Fig. 7-5. Bright yellow linen and a black-and-white Aran Islands sash mark off the place settings. Linen runners woven by Midge Dodge. (See also Fig. C-19.)

Try other combinations, some of which are shown in Figures 7-6, 7-7, and 7-8. For example:

One or two strips on a plain-color cloth.

Pattern weaves with plain-weave strips.

A wide runner overlaid with narrow strips.

Regulation place mats and strips supplementing each other.

Radiating runners for a hard-to-set round or oval table.

If your table top is of handsome wood, just a few woven strips will do, but if it is less than beautiful, cover it with many wide strips, woven in and out.

Use your collected treasures as table decorations along with your own woven pieces. As mentioned in the caption for Figure 7-5, put an Aran Islands sash over a yellow runner. Use bright woven belts as centerpieces or as overlays on a plain cloth.

Bands all in the same tones of grayed yellows and oranges but in slightly different patterns blend well on a teak table. In Figure 7-9 they are shown combined with a wide linen runner from Denmark, which is a bright orange with yellow-and-gold pattern.

Two rebozos crossed on a round or square table are attractive.

If you fear food spots, arrange the fabric so the plates are on the table itself and the runners make the divisions.

I use a lovely Japanese obi as a runner down one side of a long table for a buffet setting.

Look over your supply of textiles with a fresh eye and new thoughts, and use them in interesting new ways.

For refinements of the spontaneous idea of using woven strips, try these suggestions:

Weave several strips all in the same single color, but each one of a different loom pattern.

Plan several runners in an array of colors to complement your dishes and tabletop, then weave each runner in these colors, but vary each one by using different weights of yarn and different patterns. For example, one strip might be in fine linen, another in a nubby cotton, and others in slub linen, or mercerized pearl cotton. Patterns might be several different twills or treadled variations of Honeysuckle or any pattern you especially like.

Weave narrow widths of fabric in a whole rainbow of bright, light, and subtle colors for a broad choice when you set your table.

If you have not already woven a color blanket as a study of color relationships, you may want to, for use as a table textile as well as a color guide. There is no more graphic way to see what happens to colors when yarns are interwoven, and I earnestly urge you to weave at least one color blanket whether you make it in a table runner size or not!

Fig. 7-6. Put a narrow runner on top of a wider one. One of the black-and-white 8-harness twill samplers and a narrow bound-weaving sampler in pastel colors are shown. The knotted fringe is an added design and sampling of end finishes.

Fig. 7-7. On a long, wide rectangular table, place long runners and add place mats along the sides.

Fig. 7-8. A good solution for six places at a round or oval table: Put the plates on the cloth or the spaces between. Some strips are in Silver Star tie-up, with different overshot treadlings. Strips in Figs. 7-6, 7-7, and 7-8 woven by Ethel Jackson. (Photographs of Figs. 7-5 to 7-8 by Beverly Rush)

Brief, general directions for weaving color blankets are given. Translate them into the size you choose, which may be several square mats or two runners.

The warp and weft are identical. Prepare a warp 16 in. wide, composed of the spectrum of six rainbow hues plus black and white, each color 2 in. wide. Each weft color is woven in the same order as the warp stripes. For a long runner, each color will be woven for more than 2 in. For a square sampler, weave 2 in. of each weft color. Warp and weft stripes can vary in width, but keep them in the same progression of color. Weave this one in plain weave.

A second color blanket might be woven in loom patterns, using a lighter value of each color in the same order as the rainbow hues. For a maximum study, each color could be threaded to a different loom pattern. You can imagine the number of variations possible, in both color and pattern, across the width of fabric.

A color blanket is truly representative of the weaving craft. One that is woven with imaginative planning and design is educational and a most suitable wall adornment in the home or studio of a weaver.

Fig. 7-9. Narrow woven bands in soft yellow to orange tones with a wide linen runner of bright orange on a teak table.

The same bands shown in Figure 7-9 were rearranged for a different setting, using just the bands, which are all the same width but different lengths, so the fringes fall in different places. (Fig. 7-10.)

I took the liberty of arranging Ruth Rummler's wall hanging/sampler composed of seven strips of 16-harness point twills (see Fig. 3-17) as another table-woven textile idea. (Fig. 7-11.) Even a black and white photograph shows how effective strips in just two colors are. The strips in a soft moss green, the light-yellow dishes, and the teak table make a rich blend of colors.

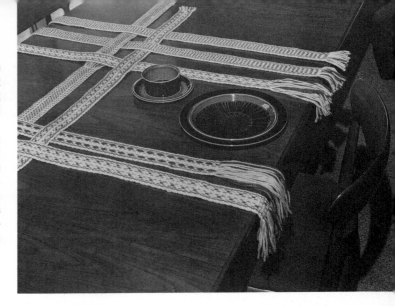

Fig. 7-10. The same bands as in Figure 7-9, but in a different woven-on-the-table arrangement. Bands woven by Sylvia Tacker. (Photographs by Harold Tacker)

Fig. 7-11. Sampler strips of 16-harness point twill treadlings in green and white illustrate the suggestion to weave strips in just two colors for table textiles. By weaver Ruth Rummler. (Photograph by Harold Tacker)

END FINISHES

When you weave a set of sample runners, plan the end finishes to supplement the overall design and furnish end-finish samples for your file. If you make the runners different lengths, some spaces on the table will be filled by the decorative fringes, as shown in Figure 7-10. Try out different warp-end finishes at each end of each strip, and you will build a large reference file of both fringes and hems.

Work the many ways of hemstitching, decorated hems, and rolled hems. Turn the edges up on the right side and sew them with fancy stitches. Practice good, plain hemming.

Allow extra warp to weave plain inches for hems, or have enough length to knot, braid, or fringe.

Beverly Rush, who photographed the runner ideas in Figures 7-1 to 7-8 had a grand time. The runners plus place mats in Figure 7-7 gave her the idea of making a bedspread from strips and rectangular mats. Try it! Also, try sewing narrow bands on the seams of joined fabric widths for large tablecloths.

As a change from the usual rectangle, weave large squares for a square table.

There is no end to where you can go with this whole plan of building a larger sampler file while setting conversation-piece tables.

LOOM-SHAPED TABLE TEXTILES

Round and oval tables pose a small problem for neat settings. If you do not want to use a full cloth, the standard rectangular or round place mats are somewhat awkward. Weave shaped mats, custom-tailored to your needs. In the same way you weave shaped clothing or upholstery, you can cut paper patterns to fit the arc of your round table and weave mats to fit. The edges will be plain selvedges, or you can add embroidery edges.

Weave a "cross" shape for a round or square table in the same manner suggested for upholstery. Also note the reference in chapter 1 to the rug woven in this fashion for a court table.

For an oval table, weave a cross with two long and two shorter arms. Weave wedges sized to a segment of your round table. Weave half-circles or ovals.

Make some mats with silverware/napkin pockets for picnic tables.

LOOM-SHAPED MATS FOR A ROUND TABLE

PARTY TIME

For buffet meals, weave "lapkins"—oversized rectangles with a pocket which you spread on your lap. Tuck silverware and a napkin in the pocket, roll them up, and stack them on the serving table.

While experimenting with small laid-in and overlay patterns, I put on a very fine warp, about 6 in. wide, of natural mercerized cotton. Each pattern example was woven in the corner of a 6 in. length. One inch of unwoven warp was left between each example, for a short fringe when the 6 in. squares were cut apart. In each section a different weft color was used. When finished, I had more than a dozen little individually designed cocktail napkins and a greater understanding of laid-in techniques.

Use your weaving time to the fullest, and use everything you weave.

Chapter 8

Weaving for and with Children

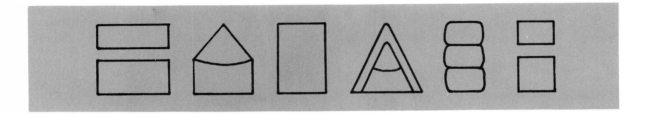

Let the kids have handwovens, too! Living with handcrafted things is to learn an appreciation for and recognition of design and craftsmanship. I firmly believe that an early awareness of colors and textures and the personal satisfaction of doing handwork is fostered by the joy of creating and using natural skills. The craft of weaving is our treasured heritage and a basic skill. Knowing about textiles has continuing application all through a lifetime. A youngster relates to and will have fun learning the names and textures, colors, shapes, and fabrics from a tactile wall hanging or play-blanket and will also learn from choosing yarns and colors for something made just for him.

In this chapter, I propose some ways to include children in your weaving plans. You can adapt the projects to your own situation and skills.

Fig. 8-1. Brian Jason's swing, woven for him by his grandmother, Ruth Rummler. (Photograph by Harold Tacker)

WEAVING FOR CHILDREN

Maybe grandmothers aren't the *only* ones weaving for children, but it does seem like it, as most of our fine examples are for grandchildren; baby blankets, shawls, and quilts are woven and gratefully used. In pretty pastels of soft yarns, they offer a perfect reason to weave patterns like crackle, canvas weave, honeycomb, or any of the loom-controlled weaves that make a light but firm fabric. Tiny ponchos, either one square with a woven slit for the head opening or made from several woven strips or squares, are useful and fun to make. One grandmother wove sleeveless easy-wearing and easy-on jackets for three youngsters. The jackets were made of a long rectangle, woven with a slit up the center front, and caught under the arm at each side. Children grow so fast that woven wearables like ponchos and vests without exacting fit will last long enough for the effort of weaving them. Weaving rugs and swings and playthings is also rewarding.

Weave with durable, washable yarns. Employ kid-proof techniques, with loops and ends secure from small plucking fingers. Weave rugs that will take it from scuffing little feet or rough use as a toga or hideout. A personalized play-rug would be amusing to plan and enjoyable to do. Weave in the child's name, the date, and other personal things like a pet or favorite toy. You can also include simple game markings and roads winding around for cars, trains, and people. Indicate paths, villages, cities, rivers and lakes by low and high clipped pile—all in simple, abstract cut-out style. The child's imagination will soar and expand if the rug only suggests objects and areas in simple shapes rather than precisely pictorial delineations.

Weave a play-pocket/wall decoration, using the pocket technique in double weave; or do it in a patchwork with small pieces left from your yardage weaving. Add some decorative stitchery and a woven band for a hanger and border. The pockets will display and stow toys. Hang a pocket low enough so the small owner can use it.

Maybe you will want to weave some small stuffed playmates or make them from yarns and woven scraps. See the Winnie the Pooh group in *Weaving Is Fun*. Kanga and Roo escaped from those pages to give you a look at a shaped figure woven on a frame loom. (Fig. 8-2.) The warp ends were darned in, and felt was put on the back. Roo is separate, of course, and comes out of the pouch. Weave in or sew on a small piece of Velcro, and sew the other part on the background cloth so that the play weaving can be pressed on or pulled off from the background. Figures like Kanga and Roo could be woven and placed in play-pockets or on a fanciful village or forest background. The sheep in Figure 8-3 might join others in a stitched or woven pastoral background. The uses of the play-pocket will change as the child grows. A pocket like this is pretty enough to help decorate a room as well as being handy for storing small treasures. A young craftsman may want to design his own wall-pocket and weave or assemble it for his own requirements.

Fig. 8-2. Kanga and Roo, woven to shape and backed with felt. By weaver Sonia Beasley. (Photograph by Kent Kammerer)

Fig. 8-3. A small woven sheep to put on a woven background or to hold. By author. (Photograph by Kent Kammerer)

Some of the tapestries woven for the Tacoma Weavers' Guild bedspread (see Fig. 6-5) suggest subjects for small tapestries. (Figs. 8-4 to 8-7.) A row of several little tapestries would be a charming addition to the wall. Quite young children themselves can manage a simplified version of pictorial weaving.

The perky ladybug in Figure 8-8 was woven on an embroidery hoop loom. The appendages were added later, and felt was sewn on the back. The bug can be pinned on a curtain or bulletin board or mounted in a frame.

For a child, as well as oldsters, Harriet Fish suggests a way to make a play-ball woven of soft cotton yarn and stuffed with nylons. After stuffing, draw up the looped warp ends at each end and you have an inexpensive plaything that is completely washable, easy and pleasant to catch, lightweight, and soft. (See Bibliography.)

Fig. 8-5. Hornet.

Fig. 8-4. Tapestries from the Tacoma Guild bedspread suggest weavings for a child's room. This one is the big fat hen.

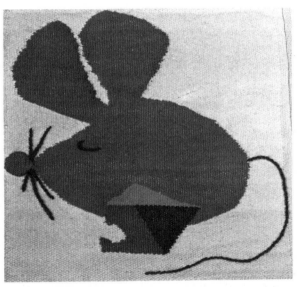

Fig. 8-6. The bright red mouse.

Fig. 8-7. Sunshine and clouds. (Photographs of the tapestries by Beverly Rush)

LEARNING WITH TEXTILES: A TACTILE BLANKET

When she was only a few months old, our grandbaby, Dawn, was very aware of the difference in fabrics that came to her hand. She patted, stroked, picked, and fingered clothing, blankets, toys, and prints with an extremely intent look of concentration. So I made her a tactile blanket—as much for my own enjoyment as spectator and weaver as for her to experience. This little experiment convinces that it would be well worth it for grandmothers and other people to assemble a small tactile blanket. On a pair of bright velvet/terry-cloth washcloths, I stitched an assortment of more than a dozen bits of material. Zigzag stitches of all sizes and colors fasten down the assortment, with some pieces folded, some stuffed, some left partly unstitched for a pocket. I included cotton prints; silk; a pile rug scrap; plastic webbing; ribbed, bumpy, and embossed cloth; nylon net with a coil of yarn underneath; and a length of rug roving stitched along the center, coiled and curving with a long knotted tag end, and, of course, some handwoven scraps! The reverse side is bright, with one washcloth wildly printed in yellow, orange, and pink, and the other one plain orange, The whole surface is quilted and lumpy from the stitching on the other side. When the blanket was placed before her as she lay on her stomach on the floor, Dawn had the very reaction I had hoped for. She quickly put out a finger, gently touched it—studied it—then touched different patches, patted and stroked—then lifted a corner to see the other side! For months she continued to study it, and this grandmother likes to think she is getting an early idea of textile textures and colors. The piece is expendable, but goes through the washer and dryer and stays in good shape, and is constantly being rediscovered all over again! If you weave a tactile blanket, make it of all sizes and colors of synthetic yarns, and use good, tight weaving so tiny fingers can't pull too much loose. Or stitch one up from all handwoven scraps in your odds-and-ends box. Add surface texture with weaves, stitchery, folding, and padding.

Fig. 8-8. Ladybug woven on a small hoop loom. Woven by Sonia Beasley. (Photograph by Kent Kammerer)

FOR THE YOUNG SWING SET

One of the most delightful weavings I have seen in a long while is the baby swing, woven by Ruth Rummler for her grandson. She sent it to me for photographing and I just happened to have an available baby in the right size for it. (Fig. 8-9. See also Fig. 8-1.) It is pictured outdoors on the roof deck, even though it is called an "Indoor Baby Swing," and can hang inside just as well. Ten bright warp colors (every color but blue) woven with a white weft give it a light, bright look.

This swing is made by a true weaver! There is no sewing or glueing—only knots and wrapping and an interlock joining made in the weaving. Many techniques are used to good advantage: diagonal twill, herringbone, tubular weave—plus braided, wrapped, and fringed warps, twined edges, and loom-shaped side pieces. Ingeniously planned and woven, the swing shows knowledgeable use of the loom. The plan for the baby swing at right gives the dimensions and shows the techniques used.

Mrs. Rummler's directions for the swing, with some revisions, are:

Fig. 8-9. Dawn enjoys the baby swing woven by Ruth Rummler. (Photograph by Harold Tacker)

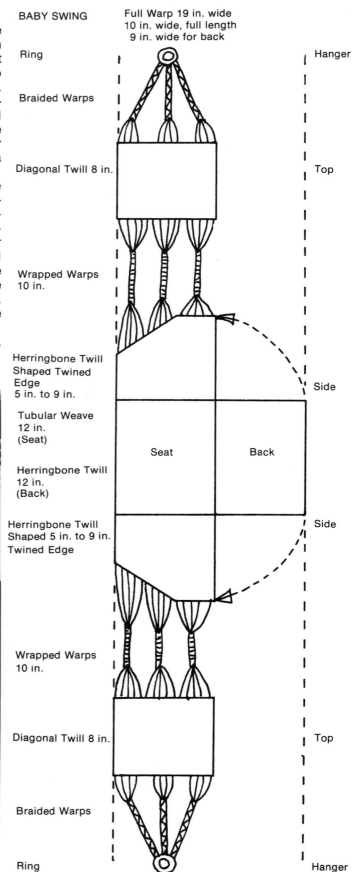

BABY SWING

Full Warp 19 in. wide
10 in. wide, full length
9 in. wide for back

Ring

Braided Warps

Hanger

Diagonal Twill 8 in.

Top

Wrapped Warps 10 in.

Herringbone Twill
Shaped Twined
Edge
5 in. to 9 in.

Side

Tubular Weave
12 in.
(Seat)

Seat   Back

Herringbone Twill
12 in.
(Back)

Herringbone Twill
Shaped 5 in. to 9 in.
Twined Edge

Side

Wrapped Warps
10 in.

Diagonal Twill 8 in.

Top

Braided Warps

Ring

Hanger

116

Sett: 10 ends per inch.

Threading: Direct 4-harness twill (1, 2, 3, 4).

Warp: 4-ply orlon. 10 colors are warped as stripes, 10 ends of each color. 10 in. wide.

Warp length: The total warp length is variable according to how and where the swing is hung. Mrs. Rummler used a warp about 4 yards long. The woven length is about 66 in., so the balance of the warp length was used for braiding the strands at the top of each side, fastening to the rings, and some was used in the weaving take-up.

Extra warp for the back section: For the 9 in. × 12 in. section woven separately for the back of the swing, which is interlocked with the seat section during the weaving, Mrs. Rummler added a separate, shorter warp. This warp was 3 yards long, 9 in. wide, of nine colors warped in stripes with one inch of each color. One end of the warp was tied to the front beam of the loom, and the other end tied to a weighted dowel and hung over the back beam. The weights put it in tension. Because this method might not work well on every loom, an alternative method is suggested. The plan of the swing indicates a warp the full width and length, and where the extra back section is woven. Arrows indicate where the back is brought up to join the two side pieces after removal from the loom. The alternative warping would use very little more length and would be done all at once.

Make one warp 4 yards long and 19 in. wide (10 in. for the seat and 9 in. for the back height). Tie the entire warp at back and front of the loom as usual. Then weave the back section as you weave the seat section, interlocking the white roving weft of the seat with the white orlon weft of the back section. The unwoven warp ends will be longer than those from the 3 yard extra warping, but since these ends will be braided and knotted for the various ties, you will have more length to work with and can make the ties longer if you wish.

Weft: 4-ply white orlon for sides, back, and top. White roving for the seat, which is tubular weave. The seat could be woven in a single layer, a pile weave added for softness, or a separate pad made.

To weave:

Treadling: Top, diagonal twill (1,2; 2,3; 3,4; 4,1).

Sides and back: Herringbone (1,2; 2,3; 3,4; 4,1; then reverse).

Seat: Tubular plain weave.

Finishing techniques to do as you weave: Wrap the warps at the sides while they are still in tension.

Wherever the weaving stops and unwoven warp continues, make a row of simple twining with the white yarn. This makes a neat-looking and protective finish. It shows well along the top of the shaped sides in Figure 8-1.

Side sections: Shape by tapering from 9 in. at the back to 5 in. at the front.

Back section: Each row of weft on this extra warp is interlocked with the tubular-woven seat weft for a smooth joining of the two sections.

Remove from the loom, assemble, and finish.

Note that the warp ends are kept in color groups and that all warp ends are put to work. In progression, they form the front tie, the back "puller," and the inside seat belt, and they fasten the woven seat to the plywood seat, as well as joining the sides and back.

Back and sides: Knot the warp ends of the back piece, in pairs, at each end. Hook these through the edge of each side piece, and knot again to form the three sides. The top three color groups are brought to the outside, braided, hooked through the front edge, and the braid continued, to make the front tie. Repeat on the other side. The ends are tightly wrapped for about an inch, with the cut ends used for a tassel.

The next two color groups across the back are knotted and brought up to the outside, braided, and tied at center back, with the ends used for a "puller."

The next two color groups are knotted in pairs and brought to the inside, knotted again in pairs, braided, and finished with two rings for a safety belt. The rings are buttonholed with yarn, and the other end is folded back and wrapped.

The last two color groups of the back are used to fasten the woven seat to the plywood base. Four holes are drilled in the plywood along each side. Divide the warps and put half down through the first corner hole in the plywood, then up through hole 2 and the woven seat. The other half goes down through hole 2 and up through hole 3 and so on with each half of the warps in all four holes, to fasten the woven seat to the wood. Knot the warps at each hole on the bottom side. Repeat at the other side of the swing seat. A tight triple knot is tied at the front corners with long ends left hanging. Figure 8-9 shows the front corner ties. The two tassels seen under the back edge are ends of the "puller." At the top, a few rows of plain weave follow the twill, then the row of twining, and unwoven warp ends, that are braided. These ends are put through a white plastic ring and brought back and tightly wrapped to form full warp fringes for a fluffy finish.

These directions are lengthy but should be easy to follow when you refer to the drawing and the photographs. The contrasting stripes make it easier to follow the paths of the warps.

JENNIFER IN A BAG

For many years and in many countries the traditional weaver's bag has been woven in fine cottons or heavy handspun wools, and with embroidered, laid-in, and loom patterns. It is as versatile as a basket, and each weaver finds her own use for it—for books, lunch, small work in progress, and a most useful and charming version is for carrying a baby. (Fig. 8-10.) When the baby outgrows it, sew up the ends, if you wish, and happily use it for other burdens, There are as many ways to finish the ends, join the sections, and finish the shoulder strap as there are imaginative weavers.

You can weave a bag like the one Garnette Johnson did for her granddaughter Jennifer. The bag has just two parts—one long, long rectangle and one wider, shorter one. These are seamed together with a long folded strip that goes over the shoulder. Jennifer's bag is a soft homespun weft on cotton warp, which makes a very sturdy, reliable fabric to hold the weight of a baby. For carrying, the shoulder strip, folded into a soft double-strap, is most comfortable. Just butt the seams together, so they will be flat, with no ridge, and sew them several times. The seams joining bag and strap should be sewn very securely also. For a larger leg opening, drop the front of the bag an inch or two lower than the back, when you put the pieces together. The warp ends are simply knotted, and at the top of the shoulder, the fabric is wrapped for a soft pad, and with long ends of fringe for decoration. Or that portion can be of pile weave, or stuffed and quilted for comfortable padding. A few good chewing toys are attached at the front with cords so baby can be amused while being toted around.

I am purposely not suggesting colors, treadlings, or many finishes, because this is a perfect project for a weaver to use and design. Some suggestions for finishing and woven treatments are wrapped warps, slit weave, weft-protector end finishes, or added surface textures. When baby has outgrown his transportation, mother can replace the toys with adult-type toys like beads or yarn embellishment and bells, and use the bag for herself. Think about making a bag like this from woven bands also—either just the long shoulder section or both parts. Remember that this is a burden bag and don't get so carried away with fanciful trims that it is a burden in itself! Make it even more useful by having a special peg on the wall to hang it on between carryings, so that it also acts as a decorative wall piece.

Fig. 8-10. Jennifer hitches a ride in the weaver's bag woven for her by her grandmother, Garnette Johnson.

You will want to size the bag to your own dimensions but the simplified drawings below show how it is put together, with suggested measurements. "A" is the long narrow rectangle which is folded lengthwise for the sides and shoulder strap. "B" is the smaller rectangle for the center bag section which is folded lengthwise. "C" shows where to sew the sections together.

TO ASSEMBLE

Finish the top edges of the center section before the two pieces are sewn together. Any of these treatments would be attractive and wear well: a hem, twining, knotted fringe, or one of the weft protector techniques.

Sew the selvedges together for about 12 in., joining A–B and A–C. Repeat on the other side, joining the center section to the other ends of the long side section. The warp fringe at the ends of the side pieces can be tied together to close when you make a handbag, but left unfastened as leg openings for the baby.

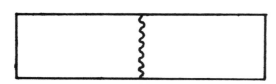

A
Suggested size: 70 in. long, 7 in. wide. Folded lengthwise.

B
Suggested length 26 in., width 7 in. Folded widthwise.

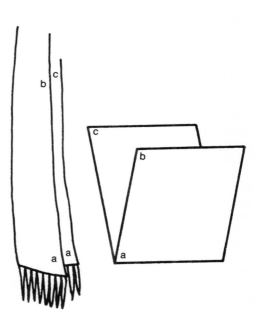

C
Match the letters and sew the shoulder piece, "A", to the center section "B". Repeat at the other side.

WEAVING WITH CHILDREN

Children are interested in handcrafting at a remarkably early age, and in the household of a weaver it is natural to work with yarns. Weave small units on a frame loom and let children participate as much as possible: helping to choose the colors, perhaps doing some rows of weaving, helping to stuff units for a puff, or choosing the occupants of the pockets in a wall panel. Keep projects small and quick—to be finished while interest remains high—but be prepared to finish it yourself. Some young ones have a short span of interest in an activity that may seem endless. It is a good idea to be making something specific—for the child or a present for someone.

At about six years of age, our son wove a scarf for his little dachshund, but weaving one for himself proved to be too big a project and he abandoned it. So, tactfully scale down big ideas to workable size. Figure C-6 in the color section shows a small, flat bag that an eleven-year-old boy wove on a cardboard loom. All on his own, he wove the two bright little figures and attached them to the green bag.

PUFF PILLOW OR QUILT

A pleasant project for an older and a younger craftsman to do together is a puff pillow or quilt. (Fig. 8-11.) Weave the units on a small frame loom, fill the individual squares with batting, and join them into a small pillow, a comforter, or expand the piece into a bedspread. Even a young child can help weave and stuff his very own floor pillow. It's a portable endeavor which is assembled as easily as crocheted granny squares or patchwork. The idea, of course, can be adapted for a larger loom and larger padded units, but the idea of weaving front and back on a frame loom works very well. Your project is finished soon after the weaving and looks like the result of a much more complicated method. Bolsters or large poufs can be made the same way. Join pads with a hinge of cloth or crochet, then stack them or spread them out flat. Use different weaves and colors for each unit, or make the units different sizes for variety. For example, two horizontal units could be joined to one vertical one. Size the units for two widths to equal one length, so they will even up at the edges. The same methods apply to assembling a quilt or a pillow. For a comforter, yarns should be finer and lighter; for a floor pillow they can be quite coarse and heavy. Dawn's puff pillow is woven of worsted-weight orlon yarn and stuffed with dacron for washability. Utilize the warp ends—either cut or loop them—for edge fringes or for trim between units. Tie warp ends so they are invisible or fringed (see Fig. 5-9), or tie double knots with

loops as shown in Figure 2-8. See some other options for finishing after the discussion of Dawn's puff pillow. The design combinations, colors, and weaves you choose can vary like a patchwork or you can plan a balanced composition of unit sizes and just a few colors. There is much chance in a project like this for very individual designing. The following instructions will help you to weave a pillow like Dawn's puff pillow. (Fig. 8-12.)

Four padded units, each one about 5½ in. × 8½ in., are joined with Palestrina stitch and have wrapped-warp handles at two corners with warp end fringe knotted together to close the other ends.

Fig. 8-11. Dawn's Puff Pillow and the small frame loom used to weave it.

Fig. 8-12. Dawn with her Puff Pillow. Woven by grandmother, Jean Wilson. (Photographs of Figs. 8-11 and 8-12
by Harold Tacker)

TO WEAVE

Loom: Canvas stretcher frame, 12 in. × 15 in.

Warp: Orlon acrylic, worsted weight. Light yellow.

Weft: The same orlon, light yellow, light and dark green-blue.

Warp the loom round and round. (See also Figs. 4-6 and 5-2.)

Sett: Four pairs per inch. (Eight ends per inch, but woven in pairs.)

Use a large tapestry or wool needle as a shuttle—if possible, a plastic one, since they are flexible and make weaving over the frame at the top much easier.

Start the weaving with a row of Oriental soumak and a row of plain weave. Use the weft doubled, in these ways: Over and under, some rows of Oriental and Greek soumak for textural interest, change colors, and play with the color changes. Try some basket weave. Weaving over and under gets a bit tedious, so your interest will be held by the variations and your product will be more sophisticated. Keep in mind the other units in order to have a harmonious whole. I wove predominantly in yellow on one half of the pillow and mostly green-blue on the other, so that when joined, they could be alternating colors; I could have used all yellow on one side and green-blue on the other. With more than four units, the choices of color placements are greatly increased. Weave all the way up the warp, on and over the frame, and down to a total length of about 18 in. Some shrinkage occurs when the tension is off, after cutting.

The closing, stuffing, and joining procedures for the four units are the same, except for the ends. Partly for exploration of other methods and partly for different end finishes, two units were prepared one way and two another. Prepare two of the units this way: First close the narrow ends by tying together pairs of warp from the back and front sections of weaving in a double knot. Clip the warps to a short, straight fringe. The opposite end is the fold. Overcast the third sides together with matching yarn. Stuff lightly with dacron batting. Sew the fourth side shut and you have a single puff pillow to join with the others into a larger pillow. Even up the fringed ends of the two units and sew together, tight and firm, with an overcast stitch.

Prepare the other two units in the same fashion, except for the warp ends. Knot the warps in pairs, tucking the cut ends in as described in chapter 5. At each corner, wrap the accumulated warp ends into tassel/handles. Sew the two units together, as just described. Bring the folded ends just together and sew firmly. Work a row of Palestrina stitch, with doubled yarn, on the long seam. Do this on each side of the reversible pillow.

OPTIONS AND CHECKPOINTS

If you prefer, weave on a longer frame, warp in a figure "8", weave on a single layer of warp, weave twice the length of the puff, and fold. I chose the small frame and weaving around, because it is an easy-to-handle portable loom.

In planning for the finished size of each puff, allow some extra width for draw-in during the weaving and extra length for some take-up by the stuffing.

For a firm base to weave against, start the weaving with two strips of cardboard and/or two rows of plain weave.

The warp at the edges, or the warp ends between the blocks, allows some unusual uses of fringe, and your units can be put together so the fringes fall in a pattern, or as stripes and edging.

If you want loops, take the frame apart and slip the weaving off. After cutting or removing, knot the warp ends together immediately and no further weft protector will be needed.

An intriguing design idea to try is to close the narrow ends by tying. This gives you a ring of weaving, and the joining can be moved around to the top of the puff or remain at the edge.

A hand-sewn joining, chosen for strength, is always preferred. However, if you need an extra strong joining, machine stitch and then work some hand embroidery over it.

Suitable joining stitches are the backstitch, closely-spaced Y stitch, chain stitch, Sorbello, or other firm, fancy methods that join.

The fold ends can all be placed at the outside edges, with the warp ends—with or without fringe—put at the center where the units are joined together.

As you weave, keep checking the width so all units will be even and equal—unless your design calls for definitely different sizes.

Put a paper or cardboard between warps for less confusion and easier selection of the top warp. It's easier on the eyes, too.

Hope Munn wove a lovely little crib quilt of very fine wool in soft shades of orange and gold. (Fig. 8-13.) The quilt is in double weave and was woven in strips and lightly stuffed as woven. The joining of the strips disappears as part of the padded squares. With no extraneous trims or patterns, the quilt is a prime example of very good design and excellent craftsmanship.

A small floor quilt for a grandson to nap on and enjoy was woven by Sylvia Tacker. (Fig. 8-14.) Fresh and bright, the white and yellow bands were woven, stuffed, and joined. To strengthen the joinings and to embellish the seams, yellow yarn was couched along the furrows made by the rounded bands.

Fig. 8-13. Crib quilt in lightly padded double weave, woven in narrow strips. By weaver Hope Munn. (Photograph by Harold Tacker)

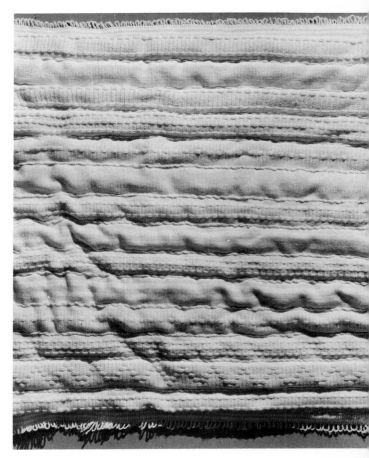

Fig. 8-14. "Karl's Quilt" is a yellow floor quilt of woven stuffed bands for a small boy who naps on the floor. Woven by Sylvia Tacker. (Photograph by Harold Tacker)

Chapter 9

Especially for Weavers

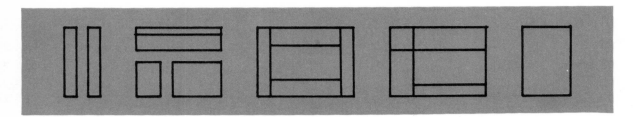

A WEAVER'S WALL

Shuttles and other tools of the weaver's trade are so handsome—usually handcrafted and cherished—so they should be on display. A very handy, workable, and useful setup for a working weaver is a weaving wall for most-used tools. It is decorative in itself and places your many choices of shuttles and other tools before you—in sight, within reach, and tidy.

Let's face it, weaving *is* an untidy occupation! Yarns on yarns build up, tools disappear, you immediately run out of cleared space, a pencil or small cartoon is deep in a yarn basket before you know it. I always start out in such orderly fashion with everything—shuttles, blunt needles, bobbins, scissors—within easy reach and sight, but in the enthusiasm that mounts, the confusion grows. A weaving wall may help you to be a bit more organized at the beginning of your working hours at least. Each weaver works out a personal system of arranging weaving apron, bench, around-the-neck scissors, and tape measure, but more ideas for organization of your materials might help too.

My weaver's wall is a very personal solution to the problem of using and storing tools of the trade. For several years the idea of a wall of tools had been nudging at me, until I devised a workable plan. Harold Tacker offered to weave the bands to my specifications and this brought the idea to completion. Figures 9-1 to 9-5 show the result. Yards of bands were woven in Persian rug wool, all in the same yellows, rusts, gold, and browns, with variations in pattern, color combinations, and widths for a harmonious whole. Sylvia and Harold Tacker even dyed some of the wool with Scotch broom to provide my favorite subtle yellow.

Fig. 9-1. The Weaver's Wall. By author. Bands woven by Harold Tacker.

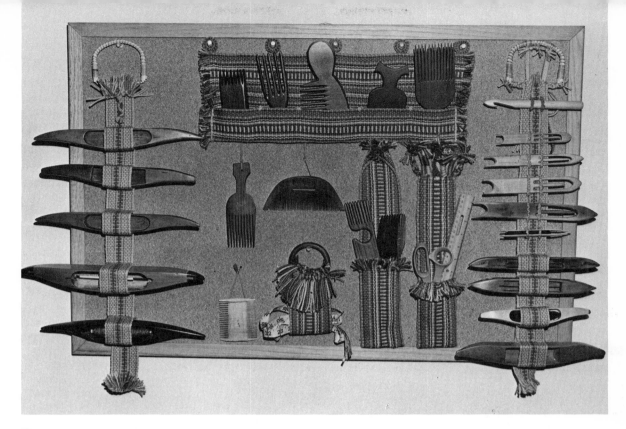

Fig. 9-2. Mostly shuttles and beaters on a 37 in. × 25 in.
cork board.

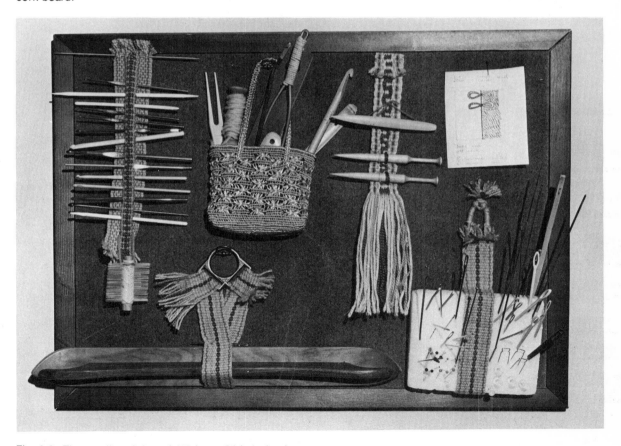

Fig. 9-3. The small cork board (19 in. × 24 in.) also has
space to pin your cartoon and threading or design notes
for weaving in progress

Fig. 9-4. Large and thick shuttles slip through slits to fit.

FABRICATION AND ASSEMBLING

The bands are 1 in., 1½ in., 2 in., and 3 in. widths. The 3 in. ones are put together for the comb pockets and vertical pockets for scissors, long tapestry combs and ruler, and a loop to hold the tape measure. Two in. bands hold shuttles and crochet hooks. One 3 in. and two 1½ in. bands are sewn together, leaving slits to hold large and thick shuttles, the flat shuttles, and various loom sticks. One in. and 1½ in. bands are holders for the ski shuttle, tapestry bobbins, and a block of Styrofoam for a pin and needle cushion. The Tackers' yardstick holder is a 2 in. band/pocket. The shuttles and other tools slip in and out easily from their slits, loops, or pockets. The first plan was to weave a 6 in. band with slits, but this would have meant much measuring and the possibility that the slits might not be just the right size, so the 3 in. band with two 1½ in. bands proved to be the best way to make the right slot for each shuttle. All of the shuttle holders were made this way: I laid the bands out flat, put a shuttle on, determined the size slot or loop needed, and pinned and sewed. I found that weaving the tools in and out, sometimes over the wide center band and sometimes under it, made the whole lineup balanced and firm. It also makes for a more interesting pattern overall.

This project was just as much fun to assemble as I had anticipated, and works as well, too. The hanging devices are both picturesque and practical, making use of handcrafted objects collected for this purpose, such as bamboo teapot handles, a bamboo ring, and part of a brass horse bridle (holding the ski shuttle). The little macrame9 "Bikini Bag" holds miscellaneous small tools. (Fig. 9-3.) Most of the smaller tools are on two cork boards, which are portable and changeable. Another enjoyable aspect was devising all kinds of end and top finishes, using weft and warp protector edges, fringes, knots, wrapping, and so on. The forest of tapestry needles from 1 in. to 7 in.—bag, sewing, upholstery, and plastic yarn needles, along with pins—easily pop in and out of the chunk of Styrofoam. (Fig. 9-3.) This corrals those numerous necessary, much-used, and rapidly disappearing needles, bodkins, and pins.

Each weaver's wall will be different, reflecting individual tool kits, situations, and working methods. Think about one for yourself. If you are like most crafts workers, you like to see a spread of mostly handcrafted and useful objects—and have them easily at hand. This idea works so well I have planned another set of holders for our working and decorative wooden spoon collection.

Fig. 9-5. The flat tools. (Photographs of Figs. 9-1 through 9-5 by Harold Tacker)

WEAVERS GUILD GROUP PROJECTS

Never underestimate the power of a guild of weavers when they propose a weaving program for the group. The Tacoma Guild's tapestry bedspread and the South Coast Weavers' Guild's screen are described in chapters 6 and 3 respectively, but I will mention a few of the other guild projects I happen to know about. Some were for learning days at meetings, some for exhibition entries, but all have something to add to a weaver's store of knowledge. Learning new weaving patterns, techniques, and ways to assemble weavings is much more enjoyable when it is part of a larger scheme, and everyone learns more by doing and observing.

Regional conferences of handweavers also yield projects for a group, and often the idea is adaptable to a single weaver's long-range weaving plan for her home. Study groups within guilds often come up with plans worth considering too.

For the Northwest Regional Conference in Vancouver, B.C., members of one guild wove small tapestry self-portraits, and it was amazing to see the likeness of each one, when compared with the photograph of the weaver! This would be a wonderfully fruitful program for a family to follow.

A study group of about a dozen weavers made a project of weaving for a summer place. Each one chose something to weave: an area rug; pillows; curtains; place mats, and so on. All objects were coordinated for color and compatability. This is just what a weaver might do in her own home: Make a long-range plan of a number of textiles to weave, then when you want to weave something, or fill a textile need, select from your planned items and colors. Going about it this way results in weaving you can use—with the probable added benefit of family helpers, the joy of creating something for your own home, and the good feeling of having projects planned and settled, waiting for the doing.

The Seattle Weavers' Guild had a workshop day planned around joining techniques, with a finished pillow for reference. Five pieces of wool fabric, chosen for their handwoven look, were given to each member for the pillow top and a piece for the back. (Fig. 9-6 shows one pillow top in progress.) Using yarns brought from home, each weaver worked on joining the pieces. In turn, six joining stitches were taught by the committee. Demonstration, drawings, overscaled examples, and a finished pillow by each committee member were ways used to teach the joinings. Help and direction were given, and some of the joined tops were quite complete at the end of the day. At the next meeting, everyone brought back handsome completed pillows. Each pillow was made entirely from one fabric, so the joinings were the important design feature. The closing seams around the edge provided four more places for hand-stitching—and four corners for tassels.

Fig. 9-6. A pillow top in five pieces, with different joinings, was the subject of a Seattle Weavers' Guild study. When completed, this joining study will have four more stitches around the edge. By author. (Photograph by Harold Tacker)

A similar workshop for making quilt squares helped solve the problem of leftover scraps. This event was truly a group effort, and it was entertaining, too. (Figs. 9-7 to 9-10.) Each member brought some handwoven swatches. After these were put on a big table, everyone dove in, extracting little gems for piecing. Members were provided with 12-in. squares of a good neutral shade of light-brown cotton. There was an embarrassment of riches—and you could go to the supply table time and again to find just the piece you needed. That day, everyone worked on the composition of pieces, then took the work home to finish. Next meeting, an array of beautiful and imaginatively sewn quilt blocks filled two tables. Padding and embroidery embellished the squares, and all were astonished at the elegant results. It is planned that the blocks will be combined into a quiltlike wall hanging or banners for the Guild's library and board room.

Fig. 9-7. A square imaginatively assembled and stitched from navy blue and white handwoven fabrics. It has the look of a blue and white tile. Note the importance of the added stitchery in the selection of squares (Figs. 9-7 to 9-10) pieced by the Seattle Guild members.

Fig. 9-8. Another single square with stitchery and design suggested by the weavings.

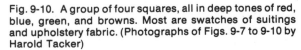

Fig. 9-9. Four squares, quite compatible in pattern and color. Each one has areas of orange plus other warm colors. Note the cat with padded face, and the stuffed tube section in the lower left square.

Fig. 9-10. A group of four squares, all in deep tones of red, blue, green, and browns. Most are swatches of suitings and upholstery fabric. (Photographs of Figs. 9-7 to 9-10 by Harold Tacker)

I was fortunate to be present at a meeting of the Detroit Weavers' Guild when it put together its exhibit for a conference—a Mondrian-inspired composition of black wood framework. As, one by one, each member put her woven section in place, we all watched the display grow, color by color, into a jewel-studded full-blown composition. Lengths of yardage were hung as background. Each piece had been woven in one color, but in different loom patterns, so each had a subtle, different texture. The fabric was stretched over a lightly padded board, making each unit a neat little package placed in its own niche. Colors were strong and clear: red, orange, blue, purple, and yellow. Impressive planning and expert execution by these talented and energetic weavers carried through a stunning idea, one that could be adapted to covering a wall in handwoven textiles.

WEAVING WITH YARN AND LIGHT

The word "use" becomes more meaningful when you experience a mental as well as a physical expansion of your vision. Look through the warp, and let the surrounding environment provide the weft—and other warps. What you see supplies pattern in space dimensions. In a window, a warp/screen will provide a softening of the glare or light while adding color and texture to the room. It also creates an ever-changing view with unlimited visual experience in contrast to a flat piece of fabric.

More and more weavers are discovering the excitement of lifting weaving from a flat plane to heights and depths, so it literally becomes free-swinging in space. Whether sculptural, structured, or in the round, such weavings require thoughtful study, a knowledge of textile techniques, and much expertise on the part of the weaver if the weaving is to be well-balanced visually and structurally and pleasing from all sides.

As an extremely brief look at this idea of using the third dimension and putting weavings into space, a few steps in degrees of freedom are shown. The warp/screen in Figure 9-11 was made to function as a screen but also provides an ever-changing view into space beyond, including changing shadow patterns in the room. (See the practical use of it in my study, Fig. 3-22.)

Multiple layers of warp hung in space can be developed far beyond this beginning, as in Figure 9-12, which has only two warps on a 1½-in.-wide bar.

Try a series of hanger bars, wide and narrow, with warps on each, then weave some, leave some unwoven, and view a changing scene through and around the space hanging.

Fig. 9-11. Warp/screen.

Fig. 9-12. Warps hung in space.

A reverse version of the warp/screen uses transparent fishline as warp. The warp seems to disappear and the weft floats in space and can provide any amount of screening. Figures 9-13, 9-14, and 9-15 have warp in just two layers about ½ in. apart, with two woven surfaces overlapping and visually related. This, too, can be expanded by installing the layers of weaving in overlapping and spaced ranks. When hung in a window or free in space, the shadows created by the moving sun add greatly to the visual experience, and the shadow pattern on surrounding flat planes expand the patterns still further, as in the study in Figure 9-15.

Fig. 9-13. Weft floats on a transparent warp.

Fig. 9-14. The weft on the second layer of almost invisible warp.

Fig. 9-15. Shadow-play adds a plane of pattern.

An extension of these ideas is a flat woven piece with openings, hung free to see through. Figure 9-16 is a new look at my tapestry "Trees" in silhouette.

Weaving in space is another way to expand your textiles beyond the two-dimensional loom. Warp in a three-dimensional structure with the warps stretched in all directions. Interweave fibers to create planes, shapes, and forms. The space weaving in Figure 9-17 is also shown in color in Figure C-14.

These are merely beginnings and ideas to stimulate exciting study and development. Do explore both the mental and the practical use of the space weaving concept, and experience the excitement of this kind of textile construction, along with the more practical aspects of weaving you can use.

Fig. 9-16. Woven trees in space.

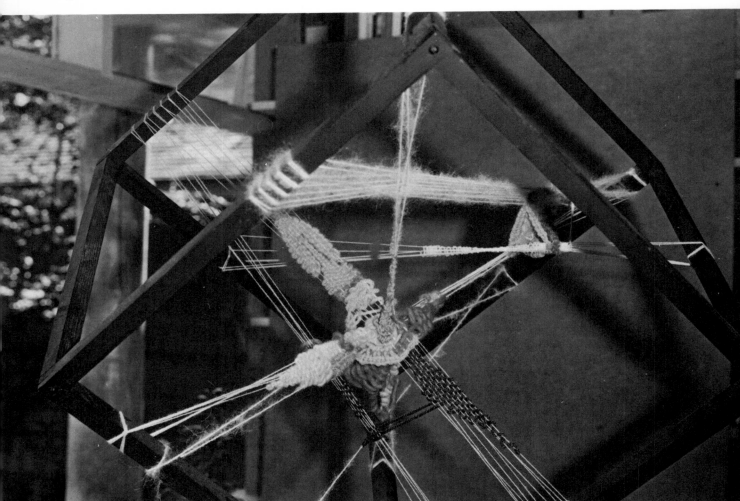

Fig. 9-17. Space Weaving. Figures 9-11 through 9-17 all by author. (All photographs by Harold Tacker)

CLOSING

In this book, I have tried to bring you some fresh and hopefully new ideas to use in your home or to use in weaving for the homes of others. I made a point of gathering what I thought were some less usual household weavings, and the ways to use them. Weavers' homes are usually brimming with handwoven textiles, such as suitably sturdy yardage made into upholstery; casements and draperies; rugs, pillows, tablecloths and mats, towels, bedspreads, afghans, throws, coverlets, baby blankets—and all kinds of flat and three-dimensional decorative hangings. The distinction and pride of work they bring to a home is very important. Weaving yards and yards of beautiful fabrics that you have designed to fit into your home is an incomparable experience. Within the limited scope of this text, there are suggestions for loom shaping and assembling small woven units; remembering the small fry; and guild activities. All these are a part of a weaver's craft-life.

Think of a room—and a home—as a whole three-dimensional composition of furniture groupings, textiles, and people. Remember that areas of quietly harmonious handwovens are the best background for accents of more intricate, colorful, or innovative weavings. Clara's woven wall covering (see Fig. 3-2) exemplifies the best kind of background to set off other weaving. The Ethnic Wall Rug (Fig. 2-3) could set a theme and color plan for a room.

Weaving to enrich your home or weaving household textiles for others is a continuing pleasure. There are so many surfaces that need or will benefit from a handwoven covering. When the fabrics are woven to blend in and relate, and are carefully made, even a houseful of handwovens won't look overdone. Coverings have a double duty; they must not only look right and enhance, but they must also work for their intended use. A rug must lie flat and clean well. Draperies must hang properly and withstand sun and cleaning. Upholstery must be elastic enough to stretch into a smooth cover and not so loose that it wrinkles. Quilts should be lightweight but warm. Weavers can create textiles that do all of the expected and necessary things—and, further, add beauty and richness to the environment—with weaving to use.

Bibliography

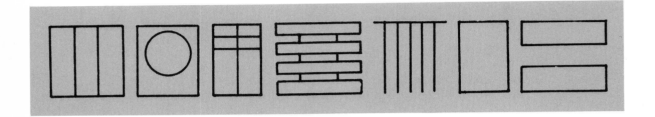

Following are a few references which will provide further information on techniques, with specific reference noted pertaining to this book.

Activities Program for Senior Citizens by Harriet U. Fish, Parker Publishing Co., West Nyack, N.Y., 1971. Information on simple and inexpensive weavings, including the play-ball.

The Art of Weaving by Else Regensteiner, Van Nostrand Reinhold Co., New York, 1970. Double Weave.

Band Weaving by Harold and Sylvia Tacker, Van Nostrand Reinhold Co., New York, 1974.

Creative Lace Making by Harriet U. Fish, Sterling Publishing Co., New York, 1972. How to do hairpin lace.

How to Make Your Own Hammock and Lie in It by Denison Andrews, Workman Publishing Co., New York, 1973. All about how to make hammocks, with some history of uses.

Needle Lace and Needleweaving by Jill Nordfors, Van Nostrand Reinhold Co., New York, 1974.

Shuttle, Spindle and Dyepot, publication of the Handweavers Guild of America, Inc., 998 Farmington Ave., West Hartford, Connecticut 06107. Four issues per year, each one full of inspiration and how-to in weaving, spinning, dyeing, and suppliers.

Stitchery Idea Book by Beverly Rush, Van Nostrand Reinhold Co., New York, 1974.

The Techniques of Rug Weaving by Peter Collingwood, Watson-Guptill Publications, Inc., New York, 1969. *Krokbragd* technique.

Techniques of Rya Knotting by Donald J. Wilcox, Van Nostrand Reinhold Co., New York, 1971. For ideas.

Weaving Is for Anyone (1967); *Weaving Is Fun* (1971); *Weaving Is Creative* (1972); *Weaving You Can Wear* (1973, with Jan Burhen); and *The Pile Weaves* (1974)—by Jean Wilson, Van Nostrand Reinhold Co., New York. For more about all of the techniques and methods discussed in this book.

Index